D1226551

chopin

compact companions

PHILIPS *Classics*

COMPACT COMPANIONS

CHOPIN

in association with CLASSIC *f*M

CHRISTOPHER HEADINGTON

PAVILION

First published in Great Britain in 1995 by
PAVILION BOOKS LIMITED
26 UPPER GROUND
LONDON SE1 9PD

Text copyright © Christopher Headington 1995
Philips Classics Compact Disc compilation ℗ 1995 Polygram Special Markets London

The moral right of the author has been asserted.

Designed by Wherefore Art? Edited by Emma Lawson.

All rights reserved. No part of this publication may be reproduced, stored in a retrieval system, or
transmitted, in any form or by any means, electronic, mechanical, photocopying, recording or otherwise,
without the prior permission of the copyright holder.

A CIP catalogue record for this book is available from the British Library.

ISBN 1 85793 655 8

Printed and bound in Singapore by Imago Publishing Ltd.
2 4 6 8 10 9 7 5 3 1

This book may be ordered by post direct from the publisher.
Please contact the Marketing Department. But try your bookshop first.

Front cover picture reproduced by kind permission of The Mansell Collection

Contents

*A drawing of
Fryderyk Chopin
(1810-49) by
Eugene Delacroix
(Mansell)*

Background and Childhood

O ne of Chopin's biographers, Camille Bourniquel, has called him the most loved, along with Mozart, of all the great composers. This is not to say that Chopin is therefore superior to, for example, Bach or Beethoven, for 'loved' is a different word from 'admired'. For some musical scholars, admiration is better than affection, because it implies judgement instead of mere feeling. Mozart, Bach and Beethoven, they point out, excelled in every field of music, both vocal and instrumental, in writing for one performer or bigger groups, and using forms ranging from the smallest pieces to operas and symphonies. Chopin, on the other hand, gave the musical world no opera, symphony or string quartet, but instead wrote mostly for solo piano and on a small scale.

The argument carries some weight. But who is to say that Shakespeare's sonnets, just fourteen lines long, are inferior to his plays, which occupy a whole evening in the theatre; or that a painter's vast canvas must be better than a miniature? They are simply different. Among Chopin's achievements, during his short career of around two decades, was that of opening up a new pianistic world. His fellow composer Robert Schumann said that his music encompassed the whole range of sound, while the writer Louis Aguettant suggested that he 'created the modern piano' and André Gide felt that until Debussy (who loved Chopin's art), music had never been so 'infused with the play of light, the murmur of water, wind and leaves'. His genius was recognized early in his life, and when he died in Paris at the age of thirty-nine, a contemporary wrote, 'The soul of music has passed from the world.'

Although Fryderyk Franciszek Chopin was born and brought up in Poland, his father Nicolas was a Frenchman from the Vosges, and the composer in his turn settled in Paris at the age of twenty-one and never returned to his native land. By doing so, he became a divided spirit. He continued to love Polish things, maintained affectionate links with his family, and while composing elegant waltzes and nocturnes which seem French in character, also penned fiery polonaises and sharp-edged mazurkas which are wholly Polish. Similarly, the letters that he wrote in French are more refined in tone than his Polish ones, which are tougher and usually more revealing. He was a reserved man who disliked discussing his feelings and musical methods; his letters and diaries, however, reveal someone who, for all his genius, was rarely at peace with himself and latterly fought a long, losing battle with illness. Even at twenty-one, he wrote of being melancholy and added, 'Why am I all alone?' Later he was to say, 'I know I've never been of use to anyone, even myself,' and elsewhere he wrote of feeling 'like an instrument from a great maker that needs mending'.

His background, however, was conducive to the early development of his talent, for his home was happy and his father reasonably well-to-do. Born in 1771 and the son of a French wheelwright, Nicolas Chopin was a native of Marainville, where the local estate was owned by a Polish count. This nobleman appears to have taken a kindly interest in the boy, and when Nicolas was sixteen his bailiff Jan Adam Weydlich took him to Poland, where he became in turn a clerk in a tobacco factory, an officer in the National Guard during a short-lived uprising against the foreign powers then ruling the country, and, finally, in 1802, a tutor in the household of the noble Skarbek family at Żelazowa Wola, a pleasant estate some thirty miles from

The interior of Chopin's birthplace with his upright piano (AKG)…

right *Chopin's parents, Nicolas and Justyna (Lebrecht)*

below ... *exterior of the house at Żelazowa-Wola (Lebrecht)*

Warsaw. There, in 1806, he married a well educated but poor Skarbek relative, Tekla-Justyna Kryżanowska. Fryderyk Franciszek, born on 1 March 1810, was the second of their four children; the others were Ludwika (1807), Isabella (1811) and Emilia (1813).

Seven months after Fryderyk's birth, Nicolas took up a post at the Warsaw High School, teaching French language and literature and moving into quarters near the school and the city's university. Fryderyk was to attend the school from 1823 to 1826, but long before this he had begun his studies at home and showed unusual gifts, writing verse at the age of six and beginning piano lessons at the same age with Wojciech Żywny, who remained his teacher until 1822. It was not long before he was recognized as a musical prodigy and called 'Mozart's successor', but Żywny kept his boyish energies on a certain rein and instilled in him a deep respect for tradition, as represented above all by Bach and Mozart. However, as far as piano technique was concerned, Fryderyk seems to have needed little help, and his father later told him, 'The mechanics of playing took you little time.'

He liked improvising at the piano, and his first written-down pieces were those he composed to play himself. A pair of polonaises, in G minor and B♭ major, date from 1817, and the first of these, dedicated to Countess Skarbek, was actually published in November of that year. Other polonaises and mazurkas followed as he reached his teens. Maybe Żywny gave him some help with these pieces, for they are surprisingly assured in style, only their brevity suggesting the composer's inexperience. All of them were Polish-inspired, and so were two Polish dances of 1818, since lost. But the young composer soon explored new areas and by the age of sixteen he had composed some Variations on a Theme of Rossini for flute and piano, and two works for piano alone called Three Ecossaises (Scottish dances) and Introduction and Variations on a German National Air.

Fryderyk Chopin made his official début as a pianist on 23 February 1818, a week before his eighth birthday, playing a concerto by the Bohemian composer Adalbert Gyrowetz (1763–1850); Żywny, also Bohemian-born, probably admired this friend of Haydn and Beethoven whose music represented a safe classical tradition. Here, opined the *Warsaw Review*, was 'a real genius'; not only did he play with ease and taste, 'but he has already composed several dances and variations which fill the connoisseur with astonishment'. The writer added, with nationalist pride, 'Had he been born in Germany or France, he would surely already be famous.'

From now on, he played occasionally in public, and the fashionable salons of Warsaw continued to applaud him. In 1823, following another concert, a critic noted that while Vienna was being astonished by the young Franz Liszt (then eleven), 'We shall not envy Vienna their Mr Liszt, for our capital possesses one equal to him, and perhaps even superior, in the shape of young Mr Chopin.'

In the summer of 1825, Fryderyk also performed on a now obsolete keyboard instrument called the aeolomelodicon, which combined features of the piano and the organ. His skill on it brought him a hearing before Tsar Alexander I of Russia on a

Chopin's first teacher,
Wojciech Żywny (Lebrecht)

As a schoolboy Chopin frequently caricatured both himself and others (Lebrecht)

visit that he made to Poland, now a satellite ruled by his brother, the Grand Duke Constantin (Alexander styled himself King of Poland); and the Tsar was so impressed that he rewarded the boy with a diamond ring. Constantin himself, who lived in the Belvedere Palace and was feared for his anger, would sometimes send a carriage for Fryderyk and require him to play. Evidently it calmed him. On one occasion he asked the young boy, 'Why do you look upwards, little one? Do you read the music from the ceiling?'

This was hardly an ordinary upbringing. Yet Fryderyk kept his head. In this he was helped by his parents, a sensible couple whom he loved and respected; an early written tribute to his father of December 1818 has the words, 'The finest concerto could not do justice to my devotion to you.' Unlike Mozart's father, who exploited his son's gifts by touring Europe with him as a prodigy, Nicolas Chopin managed Fryderyk's development with consideration and intelligence.

In 1823 Fryderyk, aged thirteen, entered the Warsaw High School (Lyceum), where his father was still teaching, and over the next three years he acquired a good general education. He seems to have enjoyed school, had a lively sense of humour and skilfully mimicked his masters (someone later said that he should have become an actor), and made several friends who remained close to him thereafter. He also showed above average ability at general school work, and after a year at school shared a fourth-form prize.

It was an invitation from a school friend called Dominik Dziewanowski that took him to the village of Szafarnia, where he spent a summer holiday on the Dziewanowski estate in 1824. From there, he sent his parents extracts from a fictitious journal that he named the *Szafarnia Courier*, which included a description

of a concert at which he ('Monsieur Pichon') played music including his own brand
new Mazurka in A minor, possibly the one that he later revised and published as his
Opus 17 No. 4. He wrote:

> *HOME NEWS. On 15 August, at a musical gathering in Szafarnia, consisting of a*
> *score or so of somebodies and nobodies, Monsieur Pichon figured in the programme,*
> *playing Kalkbrenner's concerto, which did not, however, make such an impression,*
> *particularly on the nobodies, as* The Little Jew *{the mazurka}, performed by this same*
> *Monsieur Pichon.*

Another extract from his *Courier* ten days later proves that the fourteen-year-old was
interested in singing as well as folk music, and his mention of 'Catalani' refers to the
Italian operatic soprano Angelica Catalani, who had heard him play at the age of
nine and given him a gold watch:

> *As he was passing through Nieszawa, Monsieur Pichon heard a village Catalani*
> *singing at the top of her voice as she sat on a fence. His attention was at once caught and*
> *he listened to both song and voice, regretting, however, that in spite of his efforts he could*
> *not catch the words. Twice he walked past the fence, but in vain – he couldn't*
> *understand a word. At last, overcome by curiosity, he fished out of his pocket three* sous
> *and promised them to the singer if she would repeat her songs. For a while she made a*
> *fuss, pouted and refused, but, tempted by the three* sous, *she made up her mind and*
> *began to sing a little mazurka from which the present Editor, with the permission of the*
> *authorities and censorship, may quote as an example one verse: 'See the wolf is dancing*

there behind the mountains: he's breaking his heart because he hasn't got a wife.'

A still more uninhibitedly boyish side emerges in Chopin's letters to his school friend Jan Bialoblocki. In one letter of June 1826, he writes (with more exuberance than exactness) of the two of them having

> *counted together 132 months, seen the start of 468 weeks, 3,960 days, 95,040 hours, 5,702,400 minutes and breathed through 342,144,000 seconds* ... Ecce femina, non homo. *The Headmaster has a* daughter. *Would you believe it? Yesterday they said it was a boy, today a girl ... If you saw what changes there are in our Botanical Gardens you wouldn't believe your eyes. They have laid out such shrubberies, paths and flower beds that it is a joy to walk in, especially as we have been given a key. Don't be surprised if my writing seems rather wild, for I am unwell, and if you find no mention of my holidays don't be surprised either: I'll discuss them in my next letter. If I don't send you my clavicembalistic {keyboard} trash don't be astonished – I'm like that.*

Even in boyhood Chopin was not very strong. His parents had sent him, and also his younger sister Emilia, to Szafarnia partly because they felt that a stay in the country could do them good. In fact Emilia's health was already poor, and in 1827 she died of pulmonary tuberculosis, the illness from which Chopin himself later suffered. At the time of the letter just quoted, his mother was about to take them both to a Silesian spa called Reinertz (now Duszniki), and from there he told another friend, Willie Kolberg:

They say I'm looking better. I've even put on weight and so grown lazy; you can blame that for the long rest my pen has had ... After breakfast I usually go for a walk until twelve, at which time one must have one's lunch so as to be able to go to the pump room again after lunch ... After supper I must go straight to bed, so how can I find time for writing letters? ... I do, of course, climb up the hills surrounding Reinertz and am often delighted with the view of the valleys. I'm loath to come down, as I have to, sometimes scrambling on hands and knees; but I haven't yet been where everybody else goes as I'm not allowed to ... there is a rocky height called the Heuscheuer, from which there are marvellous views, but the air at the top is so bad that not everyone can go there. I am one of the unfortunate patients who aren't allowed to ... Forgive this nonsensical scribble, wasting your time ... I'm off now to the pump room for two glasses of water and a ginger bun.

Chopin also wrote from Reinertz to his teacher Józef Elsner, born a Silesian German and now the director of the Warsaw Conservatory, who had succeeded Żywny in 1822 when Żywny admitted that he could teach Chopin nothing further:

Your kindness and the lively interest you have shown me encourage me to think that you will not receive with indifference the news I give you of my health. The fresh air and whey which I take very conscientiously have so much restored me that I'm quite changed from what I was in Warsaw ... Can you believe, sir, that there's not a single good piano here? I've seen nothing but instruments that give me more pain than pleasure. Fortunately this martyrdom won't last long: the time for my departure from Reinertz is approaching.

While this is the slightly self-conscious formality of a sixteen-year-old pupil, Chopin's letters to friends also discuss music and musicians, such as Alexander Rembieliński, mentioned to Jan Bialoblocki in 1825 after this Polish pianist returned from a stay in Paris. 'He has spent six years there and plays the piano better than anyone I have ever heard,' Chopin wrote, 'I'd need more than a page to describe his splendid talent.' Already he was dreaming of Paris, the European city with the greatest reputation for pianism, and little by little realizing that his native Poland was not the world and that his future career might lie elsewhere.

A Growing Vocation

By the time he was sixteen, Chopin had experienced a wide range of music, for besides his more formal studies, he had also, perhaps unconsciously, learned much from that of the people. He had heard it from Warsaw's street musicians, but in Szafarnia he found things which were more spontaneous and authentic, like young girls singing love songs, older women's work songs in the fields, and rowdy drinking songs floating out from the village inn. One letter to his parents, dated August 1825, shows his keen enjoyment of a harvest festival celebration on a neighbouring estate, where barrels of vodka were brought forth and rowdy dances went on late into the night: 'We were sitting at dinner, finishing the last course, when we suddenly heard from afar a chorus of falsetto voices, old peasant women whining through their noses and girls squealing mercilessly a semitone higher, accompanied by a single violin with just three strings.' To the strains of a mazurka, Chopin then danced with a Dziewanowski cousin and other partners; then he changed to playing a one-stringed double bass until his hosts decided that it was time for their young guests to go to bed.

In his compositions he continued his own integration of folk music and 'art music', but otherwise he readily accepted Elsner's guidance, for he was grateful to both his teachers and later declared that with them 'even the greatest fool would learn'. Elsner was as much of a classicist as Żywny, and more of a composer (though both wrote music), and as a violinist rather than a keyboard player, he did not teach Chopin the piano. But he soon gave him a harmony textbook, and the theory of

A contemporary engraving of a Polish harvest festival (Lebrecht)

music was important in his teaching. We do not know how well Chopin took to academic harmony and counterpoint, but there is no evidence that he resisted it in the way that sometimes happens with gifted musicians. His musical gods were to become Bach and Mozart, neither of whom might be thought sympathetic to a young romantic, and this regard lasted to the end of his life. In any case, Elsner knew that he was not to be forced into a mould, remarking wisely, 'Let him be; he's straying off the beaten track and ordinary methods, but that's because his is no ordinary talent.' From September 1826, he attended a 'composition and counterpoint' class at the Conservatory, and his official report includes the comments, '1827: Fryderyk Chopin, particularly gifted; 1828: Chopin ... remarkable talents, away for health reasons; 1829: remarkable talents, musical genius.'

Thus some of the music from Chopin's student years is as much Germanic, or at least broadly European, as Polish. The Rondo in C minor, composed when he was fifteen and published as his Opus 1, is clearly indebted to the German composers Weber and Hummel, and its opening idea, alternating just two notes, hardly foreshadows the great melodist that he was to become. The Introduction and Variations on a German National Air of 1826

A sixteen-year-old Chopin, drawn by Eliza Radziwill (Mansell) is again rather self-consciously German, although in fact the tune 'Der Schweizerbub' is probably Tyrolean. Yet alongside these pieces are others which state their Polishness: polonaises, mazurkas and a Rondo à la Mazur that refers to Mazovia, the region of the country which produced the mazurka, a folk dance in triple time.

However, one work from these years is neither German-Austrian nor Polish, and its very title is French. This is the Nocturne in E minor composed in 1827, listed as M19 in Maurice Brown's chronological catalogue of Chopin's music.

The nocturne had been invented by the Irish composer and pianist John Field (1782–1837), who latterly lived in Russia and composed his nocturnes beween 1812 and 1835. Liszt, who published the first collected edition of this music, claimed that it represented 'the origin of pieces designed to portray subjective and profound emotion', and although the same might be said of the first movement of Beethoven's 'Moonlight' Sonata (1801), Field certainly opened up an important field of romanticism. Indeed, his nocturnes were the first of many pianistic 'songs without words', with warm melody floating almost vocally above a patterned accompaniment and needing the piano's sustaining pedal to produce a rich yet delicate texture, and a mood which the French *Dictionnaire Larousse* calls 'tender and melancholy'.

Field's music was played in Warsaw by 1818 and Chopin knew it; leaving aside the fact that he could hardly have invented the name 'nocturne' independently, a comparison of the Irishman's Fifth and Ninth Nocturnes with the first and second of Chopin's Three Nocturnes, Opus 9, written in 1831, is revealing. Above all, the keyboard style is similar. In an age when most pianists were noisy virtuosos, Field was renowned for his subtlety: 'the way his melodies sang and floated' was how one

Józef Elsner succeeded Żywny as Chopin's teacher. He was also director of the Warsaw Conservatory (Lebrecht)

of his pupils described it. Later, Chopin's own playing was to earn similar praise and he was flattered when people compared him to Field, writing in 1833, 'If I were a bigger fool than I am, I might imagine I'd reached the peak of my career.' (When he did finally hear Field later that year, playing his Seventh Concerto, he was disappointed, but Field was by then a sick man and past his best.) As a regular opera goer (Elsner's wife sang in the Warsaw Opera), Chopin also owed much to hearing Italian opera singers in music by such composers as Rossini and Bellini, but Field's example prompted his nocturnes and thus his first steps into a new world of pianistic *bel canto*.

This E minor Nocturne begins and ends conventionally, with a long-breathed melody unfolding over a rippling left hand. Yet it goes beyond Field by having a stormy middle section that sounds a note of tragedy. People often assume it to be a late work or even a deathbed utterance, which its high opus number of Opus 72 (posth.) seems to bear out, but the number is only high because it was published after the composer's death.

In the meantime, he was still a student, and before he left school in the summer of 1826 his future may have become a matter of contention between his father and Elsner, with Chopin himself contributing to the argument. Nicolas Chopin wanted his son to go to Warsaw University, while Elsner thought that he should go to the Conservatory of Music. In the end, a compromise was reached: Fryderyk was to attend some university lectures while also studying at the Conservatory, where, as we have seen, his progress continued to impress.

Thus from the autumn of 1826 he settled into a new routine of study. At the Conservatory he took almost daily lessons from Elsner in counterpoint, the combining of melodic parts as in canons and fugues, and then went on to a thorough study of harmony (the use of keys, chords and chordal progressions), as well as the analysis of instrumental and vocal works by the major composers from Bach to Mozart. One might expect Beethoven to have figured in this programme, for he was then Europe's most celebrated and influential musician, but Elsner seems to have regarded Mozart as the ultimate model for a composer. As for the Warsaw University lectures, Chopin seems not to have followed these consistently, except for some by a poet called Kazimierz Brodzinski, possibly because he was an expert on Polish folk music.

These years were marred by a family tragedy. The health of his sister Emilia continued to deteriorate, as he told Jan Bialoblocki in a letter of March 1827:

We have illness in the house. Emilia has been in bed for the last month. She started to cough and spit blood, and Mamma became frightened. Dr Malcz ordered blood-letting. She was bled once, twice, then came countless leeches, blisters, synapisms {'nerve treatments'}, herbal remedies, all sorts of nonsense. During the whole time she ate nothing and got so thin that you would not have known her, and only now is she beginning to recover a little.

But Emilia died a month later, aged fourteen. The family was devastated and Justyna Chopin went into lengthy mourning. Misleading though it often is to link a composer's work with actual events, it is tempting to wonder whether her brother Fryderyk put something of this sadness into his E minor Nocturne, just three pages long but imbued with passion and ending on an elegiac note, and it seems no

Chopin's younger sister, Emilia. She died in 1827 at the age of fourteen (Lebrecht)

coincidence that he also now wrote a Funeral March in C minor.

Whatever impression this loss made on Chopin, he remained an ambitious young man and it did not disturb his musical progress. In the summer of 1827, in the countryside near Poznań, he composed his Variations in B♭ major for piano and orchestra on a theme from Mozart's opera *Don Giovanni*, the theme being that of the lilting Act 1 duet 'Là ci darem la mano', in which Giovanni woos Zerlina. He was still young enough for such naïvities as scribbling a few drawings on the manuscript as well as the comment 'This chord should sound well.' But the piano writing indicates that he was already a virtuoso player. The slow orchestral introduction elicits impressive flourishes from the soloist, and the final variations are a dramatic minor-key adagio and a lively polonaise. This was the first music with orchestra that he had written, and the orchestral writing is rather stiff, but the work was to be published in 1830 by the Viennese firm of Tobias Haslinger (as his Opus 2) and thus became his first to be printed outside Poland. The first performance was also to be in Vienna, taking place in August 1829 with the composer at the piano. Today, when we know Chopin's greater music, this set of variations is usually thought of as merely promising, but it was a landmark in his development. In 1831 it was to attract the attention of Chopin's German contemporary Robert Schumann, who called it a work of genius. It was also noticed by the *Gazette Musicale de Paris*, which declared that it announced this young composer's gifts 'with as much precision as felicity'.

Travel Abroad

Approaching his eighteenth birthday in March 1828, Chopin continued to make great strides as a pianist. During April, Hummel, a superb pianist as well as a composer, visited Warsaw to give two concerts and Chopin was introduced to him, probably by Elsner, and played to him; this genial man was impressed enough to follow his career thereafter. Chopin now composed his first extended work in a classical form, a four-movement Piano Sonata in C minor, Opus 4, which he dedicated to Elsner. Possibly by now he was becoming a little restive under his guidance, directed as it was towards a tradition now upheld by such composers as Hummel and Moscheles, worthy men but lacking genius. At any rate, this Sonata, now rarely played, is unconvincing, abounding in rhetoric but lacking individuality despite the unusual metre (5/4 time) of the slow movement. Chopin sent it to the publisher Haslinger, but Haslinger did not set about printing it until some considerable time later, by which time the more experienced composer had lost interest in his 'old Sonata'.

His Trio for piano, violin and cello (Opus 8) has a similar four-movement form and dates from the same year. This is of more interest, although his unease with the medium is borne out by his questioning later whether he should have used the viola instead of the violin, 'as the first [highest] string predominates on the violin and in my Trio it's hardly used: I think the viola would go better with the cello'. The finale, in the style of a krakowiak (a lively folk dance), has an authentic Polishness, and the dedicatee, Prince Antoni Radziwill, who admired and encouraged Chopin's

A watercolour of Cracow-Warsaw, by Chopin (Lebrecht)

art, wrote him a warm letter of thanks.

This busy year also saw the composition of a real krakowiak, the Krakowiak: Grand Concert Rondo in F major, Opus 14, again for piano and orchestra, plus a Grand Fantasia on Polish Airs for piano and orchestra, Opus 13, and a Rondo in C major for two pianos. The Trio, Fantasia and Krakowiak were all to be published between 1832 and 1834, each of them by three firms, Kistner in Leipzig, Schlesinger in Paris and Wessel in London.

Chopin spent some weeks of that summer in the country on an estate (Sanniki) belonging to friends, but found time there to write his Rondo in C major. He was back in Warsaw by August, and his letters of the time demonstrate his lively interest in the operas which he saw at the city's opera house. He could be wildly enthusiastic, but also highly critical: he saw Rossini's *Otello*, now largely forgotten because of Verdi's later and greater opera on the same story, and thought the performance so poor that he would willingly have strangled the cast. Similarly, after seeing the same composer's *Barber of Seville*, his comment (in a letter of 9 September 1828 to his friend Tytus Woyciechowski) was,

All day long I rubbed my hands in anticipation, but on the evening itself, had it not been for Madame Toussaint I could have murdered Colli. He acted so much the Italian low comedian and sang so much out of tune that it was terrible.

In the same letter he declared, 'Yesterday [Weber's] *Freischütz* was shockingly badly performed. The chorus members came in a quarter of a beat after each other'.

The other news that he told Tytus was exciting: he had been invited to go to

Berlin by his father's friend Professor Feliks Jarocki, a zoologist attending a scientific congress there. He was thrilled, and hoped that Prince Radziwill, whom he expected to be there, would introduce him to the city's musical figures (as it happened, the Prince was in Poznań, and he saw him on the return journey). 'Five days in a stage-coach!' he told Tytus. 'If I happen to get ill I'll return by special coach and let you know.'

He and Jarocki left Warsaw on 9 September and duly arrived at Berlin's Kronprinz Inn, and in his three weeks there Chopin saw 'with great satisfaction' several operas, among them Spontini's *Ferdinand Cortez*, Cimarosa's *The Secret Marriage* and Onslow's *Le colporteur*. At the Singakademie he heard Handel's 'Ode on St Cecilia's Day', which much impressed him: this, he told his family, was something that approached his ideal of great music. He never lost his respect for Handel, and when, later, his colleague Mendelssohn showed him more of Handel's work he felt 'a truly childlike joy'. He did not meet Mendelssohn during this visit, however, for on the one occasion when he found himself in his presence, and Spontini's too, he was too shy to introduce himself.

But he spent pleasant hours in Schlesinger's music shop; and, on a visit to a library with Jarocki, was excited to see a letter from the Polish patriot Tadeusz Kościuszko (who had led a rebellion against foreign rule in 1794) being copied by a local scholar. He and Jarocki helped by reading and translating the words of 'our hero'. At the end of Jarocki's conference, there was a banquet at which Chopin wryly noted that the participants had learned much of the science of eating, drinking and singing; the ceremonies even included a performance of some new music composed for the occasion, Mendelssohn's festival cantata 'Begrüssung'. Though he thought

A nineteenth-century engraving of Warsaw, Poland (AKG)

Berlin orderly but charmless, the visit had been fruitful and whetted his appetite for more foreign travel. Shortly before leaving for home, he told his family, 'What things I shall have to tell you as soon as we meet again!'

(On the return journey to Warsaw the stage-coach stopped to change horses at a village called Sulechow, and as there was a delay most of the passengers went into the inn. There, surprisingly, Chopin found a good piano and began to play. When the coachman announced that they could depart, no one wanted to leave. Food was set before the travellers, and the elderly village organist declared, 'If Mozart had heard you he would have cried, bravo!' Finally, Chopin was carried in triumph to the waiting coach.)

Back in Warsaw, he began his final year at the Conservatory. According to the syllabus, this was to be 'devoted to practical exercises', in other words chiefly composition. Clearly Elsner was now happy for him to concentrate on Polish themes, for he wrote his Grand Fantasia on Polish Airs and Krakowiak, and, as 1829 began, two Polish songs to poems by Stefan Witwicki, called 'There where she loves' and 'The Wish'. These were his first vocal compositions, and it seems certain that Elsner, himself the composer of a hundred songs, encouraged him to try his hand at songwriting. But song form does not seem to have strongly attracted him, and the nineteen songs that he wrote between 1829 and 1847, all to Polish words, are rather ordinary. In his lifetime he published none of them. After his death, seventeen were published as his Opus 74, but there is no connection to make them a cycle. The other two (called 'Charms' and 'Reverie') came out only in 1910.

Piano music was a different matter. During 1829, in his small studio at the top of the household, he composed mazurkas, waltzes and polonaises. He also wrote a set of variations entitled 'Souvenir de Paganini', evidently thinking that their theme was by that Italian violinist-composer, whom he had heard in Warsaw that summer; but it is a folksong called 'Carnaval de Venise'. This piece and the waltzes suggest that, musically speaking, he was now looking outwards towards Italy, Austria and perhaps France – for the Viennese waltz was already popular in France and Chopin's have a Gallic grace. The amazing thing about these pieces, written before he was twenty, is that they already show the unmistakable Chopin personality and in no way reveal themselves to be early works.

Equally Chopinesque, but still more impressive, are the four studies which date from October and November 1829 and were to become Nos. 8–11 of his Twelve Studies, Opus 10. This was pianistic writing of quite a new kind, highly resourceful and brilliant, yet at the same time subtle. The awkward hand positions of the F major Study, the left-hand stretches of the F minor, the cross-rhythms of the A♭ major and the enormous right-hand chords of the E♭ major are remarkable not only for their innovation but also because they are practical, even if only for pianists possessing a virtuoso technique. Beyond that, we find musical invention that completely belies the composer's youth and inexperience, the four pieces displaying vigour and charm, agitation and passion, elegance and wit, and a rich songfulness. Indeed, it is here, rather than in the songs, that Chopin first demonstrated his remarkable individuality as a melodist, and pianists who perform his music must be able to make their instrument sing. From now on, he recognized his vocation as that of a composer for one instrument rather than many, making personal statements rather than public utterances, with the only instrument which could both storm the heavens and breathe the gentlest of love songs.

As Chopin approached the end of his Conservatory course, his father knew that the time had come for him to 'smell new smells', as he put it. That meant travel, and on 13 April 1829 Nicolas Chopin wrote to the Minister of Education, Count Grabowski, petitioning him for funds to make this possible. 'May it please Your Excellency', he wrote:

Having been employed for twenty years as a teacher at the Warsaw High School and being convinced that I have fully performed my duties to the best of my ability, I venture to address a modest request to Your Excellency and beg for your gracious intervention with the Government, a favour which I shall regard as the best possible reward for my efforts.

I have a son whose innate gifts for music call for further development in this art. His Imperial Majesty Alexander, of blessed memory, Tsar and King of Poland, most graciously deigned to reward him with a precious ring as a token of His satisfaction when he had the honour of being heard by the Monarch ... Finally, many respectable persons and connoisseurs can support the view that my son might become a credit to his country in his chosen profession if he were given the opportunity to pursue his studies to their proper completion. He has completed his preliminary studies, in witness whereof I may refer to the Director of the Musical High Schools and University Professor, Mr Elsner. All he now needs is to visit foreign countries, namely Germany, Italy and France, to perfect himself according to the best models.

Since my modest resources, based solely on my salary as a teacher, are insufficient to cover the expense of such a journey lasting perhaps three years, I beg to submit to Your Excellency the Minister a request that the Administration might draw from the fund which has been placed at the Viceroy's disposal some contribution towards my son's expenses.

I am, with the greatest respect, Your Excellency's humble servant
Nicolas Chopin, Assistant at the Warsaw High School.

At first it seemed that Nicolas's wish would be granted. The minister himself could not authorize it, but he passed on the request to the Polish treasury authorities with his own recommendation for 'a yearly grant of 5,000 zlotys for the promising youth'. However, two months later Nicolas heard that his petition had been turned down, and the official recommendation, which he did not see, stated that 'public funds cannot be used for the support of this class of artist'. But he remained confident that funds would be found to enable his son to travel; perhaps he had already made some provision for it and the petition did not truly reflect his finances.

As for Chopin himself, he was now nineteen and full of ambition. On 20 July, he took his final music examinations with considerable success. As well as writing his official comment concerning his pupil's 'genius', Elsner also wrote in his diary that Chopin's 'astonishing' playing and compositions had 'opened up a new era in piano music'.

Departure for Vienna

On 21 July, Chopin left Warsaw for Vienna, on what looks to have been precisely the foreign travel that Nicolas planned and that Fryderyk himself desired. However, this trip began as a touring holiday: with some friends, Chopin visited Cracow and its surroundings, including the Ojcow Valley and the Wieliczka salt mines (more picturesque than the name suggests), enduring the hardships of country travel in those times, which included their simple carriage bedding down in a stream during a rainstorm.

Chopin had career reasons for visiting the Austrian capital and took several compositions with him. Soon after his arrival on 31 July, he made contact with the publisher Haslinger, to whom he had already sent the score of his 'Là ci darem la mano' Variations and First Piano Sonata. Haslinger had not yet responded, but Elsner had written to tell him of Chopin's visit to Vienna, and as soon as Chopin visited him and played the Variations, he decided that the young Pole's music would make a stir and sell. He invited Chopin to dinner and promised to publish the Variations within a week. (Chopin could not believe him, and they actually came out six months later.)

At Haslinger's house Chopin also met Count Wenzel Gallenberg, the Director of the Kärntnertor Theatre, who in turn invited him to play the Variations there on 11 August (though without receiving a fee, as he noted in a letter home). This he did, thus making his Viennese début both as a pianist and as a composer. 'Everyone here says that it would be a great loss to Vienna if I left without being heard; I simply

Vienna: The Kärntnertor Theatre (on the right) (Lebrecht)

can't grasp it', he wrote proudly to his parents. 'I don't know what it is, but all these Germans [probably meaning German speakers] are amazed by me, while I'm amazed at them being so amazed! ... [the journalist] Blahetka says I shall be a sensation, for I am a virtuoso of the first rank, to be counted alongside Moscheles, Herz and Kalkbrenner.'

Another enthusiast for his music was the operatic conductor Wilhelm Würfel, who declared that 'the Viennese are hungry for new music'. Chopin appreciated his support and told his parents, 'He has made all the arrangements [for the concert], will be at the rehearsal, and takes a sincere interest in my appearance before the public.' Even the local piano manufacturers competed for his interest: 'Stein is most kind and friendly but I shan't play on his piano, I prefer Graff's ... I have selected a Graff piano for my concert.' He told his parents, 'I hope that God will be with me – don't worry.'

In fact, not all went smoothly. The concert was supposed to include his Krakowiak as the fourth item, following the 'Là ci darem' Variations as the second, but in rehearsal the orchestra proved inadequate (they, in turn, complained that the instrumental parts in his handwriting were insufficiently clear) and he substituted an improvisation. Four days later, after the concert, he reported that although the improvisation 'did not turn out particularly well', the whole affair had been a success, and especially the Variations. 'As soon as I appeared they started clapping and the applause after each variation was so loud that I couldn't hear the orchestra ... the journalists have taken me to their hearts ... the stage manager encouraged me so much that I wasn't in the least nervous.' One lady was overheard saying that she thought his appearance unimpressive, but that remark he could scorn: 'If that's all that's wrong I've nothing to worry about.'

More importantly, however, Chopin's playing was already seen as unusual, as he noted in the same letter:

In general, people think I play too quietly, or rather too delicately for those who are used to the banging of Viennese pianists. I expected to find this reproach in the paper because the editor's daughter bangs frightfully. It doesn't matter. There's always some kind of 'but', and I prefer that one to having it said that I play too loudly ... I am curious to know what Mr Elsner will say to all this. Will he be displeased that I have played? But really they insisted so much that I couldn't say no.

In the meantime, a second concert in the same hall was quickly arranged for 18 August, and this time the Krakowiak was performed, with success. 'All admire the beauty of this composition,' Chopin told his parents proudly the following day. 'Things are going *crescendo*, just as I like it.' He was delighted to be so fêted, and to meet Vienna's musical celebrities: one was Beethoven's pupil (and Liszt's teacher) Carl Czerny, with whom he played piano duets, and another was Beethoven's preferred violinist and quartet player Ignaz Schuppanzigh. But when he told Schuppanzigh that he wanted to study in Vienna, the older man said that Vienna had nothing to teach him. 'Such things are just compliments, but nice to hear,' he noted, 'They refuse to regard me as a pupil.' Count Lichnowsky, 'Beethoven's best friend', had him to tea and gave him a letter of introduction to his sister in Paris: 'He could not compliment me enough.' On this happy and fruitful visit, he also saw a number of well-performed operas.

He left Vienna after his second concert and a promise from Haslinger to publish the Variations 'so that the musical world should have them by the autumn'. There were 'tender farewells, and after all the fuss and with many promises to return, I climbed into the coach'.

Now he went on to Prague, arriving after a bumpy journey on 21 August, seemingly still with at least one friend, since in a further letter to his family he uses 'we' rather than 'I' in describing it. He had called Vienna pretty, but found Prague even more beautiful. Armed with letters of introduction from Würfel, he met musicians and impresarios who invited him to play; but he was only staying for three days and hesitated to do so, remembering that the city was not always kind and that 'even Paganini was snubbed here'. By 26 August he had reached Dresden, to use a further letter of introduction to Baron von Friesen, the Saxon court's Chamberlain, who received him civilly. This was the last stage of his tour, during which he saw a performance of Goethe's 'frightening but powerful' drama, *Faust*. He then set off on his return journey to Warsaw, arriving home on 12 September.

At home, one thing instantly displeased Chopin. He had told his parents that they should see a critique of his Viennese concerts in the Polish papers before his return; and when they did so at the end of August the piece had seemed half-hearted in its praise. He was also bored. For one thing, he had completed his studies and found that he had little to do; for another, many of his friends were out of town, in particular his closest confidant Tytus Woyciechowski, who was on his family estate at Poturżyn. He found, too, that the political climate had become uneasy: after the death in 1825 of Tsar Alexander, his successor Tsar Nicholas I had stamped upon Polish national feeling, closing colleges and imposing censorship, and a feeling of

Konstancja Gladkowska - the first romantic attachment in Chopin's life (Lebrecht)

rebellion was in the air throughout Poland.

However, he made himself start work on a big new composition, his Piano Concerto in F minor. He met fellow musicians, and sometimes played, at the publisher Brzezina's music showrooms, which served his profession as a kind of club and coffee house. Another meeting place was the home of the piano teacher Joseph Kessler, where Chopin and others tried out new music by composers such as Spohr, Hummel and Beethoven, whose last piano trio, the 'Archduke', deeply impressed him ('I've never heard anything so great – in it Beethoven makes fools of us all'). He also kept up his regular attendance at the opera.

But he was restless. On 3 October, he wrote to tell Tytus that Prince Radziwill had invited him to revisit Berlin, but that he wanted to return to Vienna: 'I shan't stay in Warsaw, but go where things take me, wherever that may be … I ought to return to Vienna, where I made my début and have promised to return; one of the papers wrote that a longer stay there would be of great benefit to my career. You must know this.'

This letter also mentions the first serious romantic attachment in his life. Konstancja Gladkowska was a singing student at the Warsaw Conservatory whom he had first seen, and heard, earlier in the year. She had dark hair and a quiet, thoughtful expression, and though he seems to have felt an immediate attraction he made no approach and she remained unaware of it. He told Tytus: 'I'm perhaps unlucky already to have found my ideal, whom I've served faithfully for six months without saying a word, whom I dream of and about whom the Adagio of my Concerto is written, and who this morning inspired me to write the little waltz I

Chopin was a frequent visitor (and performer) at Prince Radziwill's residence (Lebrecht)

now send you.' This is his Waltz in D♭ major, Opus 70 No.3.

To these words, however, he added mysteriously, 'Notice the place marked with a cross; no one but you knows of this,' and his letter ends with the words, 'I'm sorry I sent you that waltz, which might make you angry with me, but I swear I only wished to please you, you know how very fond of you I am.'

His relationship with Tytus has been the subject of speculation. Certainly he expressed his affection for him strongly, even in phrases such as 'I love you to madness', 'I know my love for you is hopeless', and 'Give me your lips', and for this reason some writers suspect a sexual component in the friendship. But these sound less startling in Polish, where flowery language is common, and Chopin's Polish biographer, Adam Zamoyski, states that they need not imply more than ordinary affection. Zamoyski also argues that Chopin, not daring to confess his love to Konstancja, did so to Tytus instead. But he also concedes that his letters to Tytus 'contain passages of extraordinary sensuality ... nothing is, of course, impossible ... some of the letters read almost like love letters'. Unfortunately, we lack letters from Tytus which might give a further clue. Whatever the case, there is nothing like this in his correspondence with other male friends.

On 20 October, he left Warsaw to visit Prince Radziwill at his estate near Poznań, where the image of Konstancja was temporarily dispelled by the charms of the two young princesses – a paradise with two Eves, he told Tytus, where he composed a Polonaise in C major for the cello-playing prince and one of these 'musical and sensitive' girls. 'I wanted Princess Wanda to learn to play it [the piano part]; I was giving her lessons at the time. She's young, seventeen, and pretty, and it was a real pleasure putting her little fingers on the keys.'

A pencil drawing of the composer by Eliza, Prince Radziwill's daughter (Lebrecht)

Although he felt he could have stayed longer, he returned to Warsaw after some weeks to continue work on his F minor Concerto, play at his home with Żywny and Elsner for his father's name-day (6 December) and perform in a public concert thirteen days later, improvising so brilliantly that the press were more enthusiastic than ever. The *Warsaw Courier* declared, with patriotic pride: 'Mr Chopin's works unmistakably bear the stamp of genius: among these is said to be a Concerto in F minor, and it is hoped that he will delay no longer in confirming our convictions that Poland too can produce great talent.'

Not only did he have to finish the Concerto, he also had the wearisome task of preparing the orchestral parts. It was not until February 1830 that he could try out the new work with an orchestra, and a private première took place on 3 March with Chopin at the piano and Karol Kurpiński conducting. Since this happened in the Chopins' large living room, the orchestral strings were doubtless small in number: even so, this room must have been spacious to accommodate a piano and an orchestra, to say nothing of the audience. The concert also included his Fantasia on Polish Airs. The critic of the *Warsaw Courier* now dubbed Chopin 'the Paganini of the piano', and another reviewer found 'genius … everyone was moved by these works … Mr Chopin must not hide his talent, even if he must prepare to hear voices of envy'.

This successful event was followed by a sold-out public concert on 17 March in the National Theatre. During the first half, in a way that seems odd today, the first movement of the Concerto was separated from the other two movements by another work altogether; the Fantasia on Polish Airs came after the interval. Again, reactions were unanimously favourable, although Chopin's piano proved rather soft-toned for the 800-seat hall. Once more, people compared Chopin to Mozart, and a repeat concert was arranged for 22 March; this time he played a Viennese piano with a bigger tone which sounded more effective. One critic declared that what he heard seemed simply to say, 'It's not me, it's music!', and another identified a major characteristic of Chopin's style:

> *He plays with the good manners of a well-bred person who may know his own importance but remains unassuming, knowing that, if he chose, he has the right to everything. His music is full of expressive feeling and song, putting the listener into a state of subtle rapture, recalling to his mind all the happy events he has known.*

Not everything was so happy. The comparison of Chopin with Mozart evoked resistance, particularly among enemies of Elsner. Chopin was upset when a young local musician called Antoni Orlowski made his themes into dance tunes. 'Tortured' by stage fright before every concert, as he told Tytus, he now found that even success had its drawbacks, writing, 'I no longer want to read or listen to what anyone writes or says.' He also confessed to an 'unbearable melancholy … I've never been so depressed'.

But he soon recovered his spirits, and was already composing another piano concerto, this time in E minor, describing it to Tytus in a revealing way in a letter dated 15 May. Significantly, he had already told Tytus, who was himself a pianist, that he had taught him 'how to feel music' and, 'I say to my piano what I'd like to be saying to you' and even, 'My new Concerto in E minor will be valueless to me until you've heard it.' Never again was he to seek this kind of approval for his music. He wrote:

The Rondo {finale} of my new Concerto isn't finished, I must be in the right mood for that … {The Adagio} is rather a Romance, calm and melancholy, like someone looking gently towards a place calling to mind a thousand happy memories, a kind of moonlight reverie on a lovely spring evening … Write and tell me when you'll next be in Warsaw, you don't know how fond of you I am and can't show it, though I've long wished you could know. Oh, what I'd not give to press your hand! You'd never guess, half of my miserable life.

But what of Konstancja? Little had happened to bring them closer, although they met from time to time in musical circles. It may be that Chopin's fame, which both excited and embarrassed him, was actually a barrier; in any case, he was still only twenty and uncertain both of his feelings and his ability to express them, save on paper and in music: some passionate songs dating from this year may reflect his love for Konstancja, and so may a piano Nocturne in C# minor marked 'with great expression'. In September 1830 he told Tytus, 'I could go on hiding my pathetic and clumsy passions for another two years.' In any case, Konstancja now acquired a rival when he developed an admiration for a visiting German soprano, Henrietta Sontag, and started calling on her at her hotel. She was 'not beautiful, but attractive in the highest degree', he told Tytus, with an 'extraordinary cultivated voice ... her scales, particularly chromatic scales, are unsurpassable'. He heard Sontag give an informal lesson to Konstancja, who was now beginning her professional career as a singer, in the presence of her teacher Carlo Soliva, and tell her that her voice was incorrectly produced. But when he heard Konstancja make her operatic début a few weeks later, he admired both her singing and her acting.

In July, Haslinger's published version of his 'Là ci darem' Variations finally arrived and he played them at a smallish concert, and in the following month he finished his E minor Piano Concerto. Again it had a private première, on 22 September, before the official first performance in the Warsaw City Hall on 11 October. Chopin's reasons for this procedure are explained in a letter to Tytus (21 August) in which he wrote, 'I must try out my Concerto, now that the Rondo is finished', suggesting that he was still not fully confident in his orchestration and wished to check it before committing the work to a public presentation. In fact, as he doubtless knew, it was markedly inferior to his piano writing. Soon after this, he seems to have decided that it was not for him, for he wrote only one more work with orchestra, a Polonaise in E♭ major dating from 1831. This City Hall concert was another success, and he declared that he 'had never been so comfortable when playing with an orchestra'. This time, Soliva conducted, and Konstancja performed an operatic aria, 'beautifully dressed in white, with roses in her hair', as Chopin later told Tytus.

Well before the Concerto's première, he had already made up his mind to travel again to Vienna. On 25 October, he visited Konstancja to say goodbye, and she wrote in his album: 'Never forget that we Poles love you; others may appreciate and reward you more, but they can never love you more.' Little could she guess that at some later date he was to add, in pencil: 'Oh yes, they can!' A week later, his friends gave him a farewell dinner at which there was singing, playing and dancing. The next afternoon, that of 2 November, he said goodbye to his family and set off by the public coach, which was then stopped after passing the city gates by a group of musicians, for Elsner had come with a small choir to sing some music that he had specially written for the occasion. 'May your talent bring you fame wherever you go, yet still your heart will remain with us.' There were many handshakes, and probably some tears; yet no one could have known that Chopin was never to return to his native land.

Vienna

Chopin was not travelling directly to Vienna, however. Nor was he travelling alone: Tytus Woyciechowski joined him at the first halt, a place called Kalisz, and together they visited the Saxon cities of Breslau (now Wroclaw) and Dresden. At Breslau the young musician managed to get himself included in a concert and played two movements of his E minor Concerto, although in Dresden he confined himself to renewing musical contacts and attending a soirée given by a lady pianist, where he was impressed by the guests' display of bald heads and, on the ladies' part, busy knitting needles. He also renewed his friendship with Augustus Klengel, an organist and composer whom he had first met in Prague the year before. After a week in Dresden and a stopover in Prague, Chopin and Tytus reached Vienna on 23 November and took rooms at the Stadt London Hotel, although moving soon after into another inn and finally into rented accommodation in the Kohlmarktstrasse, near the city centre.

Several people remembered him with affection, for on the day after his arrival Hummel called to offer a welcome and he soon renewed his contacts with Würfel and Czerny. He also lost no time in visiting his publisher Haslinger. But here he was disappointed: contrary to his expectations, Haslinger had not yet published his C minor Piano Sonata and his 'Schweizerbub' Variations. Probably he had failed to make money with the 'Là ci darem' Variations. Whatever the case, he showed little interest in Chopin's new piano concertos, saying only that he might take one if the composer would forgo payment.

Accustomed to success as he was, Chopin was upset. He remembered that Klengel and others had encouraged him to be practical in his business dealings, and told his parents in a lengthy letter, dated 1 December:

Haslinger is clever, and quite nice to me, but wishes to appear casual in order to get my compositions free. Klengel was surprised to hear that he has not paid me for my {'Là ci darem'} Variations. Perhaps he thinks that by his pretending to treat my pieces lightly I'll take him seriously and hand them over for nothing. But I'm through with giving things for free, and now it's 'pay up, you beast!'

Whatever he expected, he was now to learn that Vienna's artistic affections were fickle. He was also put out by encounters with local bankers, from whom he sought a loan to fund his stay:

Two days ago I went to Stametz's bank, where in spite of my letters of introduction I was received like any ordinary individual coming to draw cash – I was only handed a form to give the police to get a visitor's permit ... At the same time I went to Mr Geyermüller's, since Tytus has 6000 zlotys deposited there. Having noted my name, without bothering to read the rest of the letter, he said 'that he was pleased to meet such an artiste as myself but would not advise me to appear in public, since there are so many good pianists here that one needs a big reputation to achieve anything'. He ended by adding 'that he can offer me no assistance as times are so bad'. I had to swallow all this with my eyes popping out of my head! I let him finish his tirade and then told him that I really didn't know whether it was worth my while to perform, since I'd not had time

to call on any important people, or the Ambassador {the Russian Countess Tatischeff},
to whom I had a letter of introduction from the Grand Duke in Warsaw, etc. You
should have seen his face then! I left apologizing for interrupting his business. Just wait,
you – Jews!

This cool reception from Vienna's bankers was perhaps partly linked to the current political situation. Austria, Russia's ally, had long known of the growing anti-Russian feeling in Poland, and while she preferred to remain aloof, she feared the kind of revolutionary movement that had already thrown France into decades of instability. Poles were no longer popular, as Chopin learned when, in his favourite restaurant, he overheard the remark that 'God made a mistake in creating Poland'.

Then, on 29 November, six days after his arrival in Vienna, Warsaw rose up in an armed insurrection against Russian rule. The Polish rebels failed in their attempt to kidnap or kill Grand Duke Constantin, but succeeded in disarming some of Russia's occupying troops. The news reached Vienna on 5 December, though in a confused form, and after a long and emotional discussion between Chopin and Tytus, the latter decided to return to Poland. Chopin, on the other hand, was to stay in Vienna, and with Tytus gone, he moved into smaller accommodation higher in the same building. There, he soon fell prey to loneliness and anxiety about his family and friends, as we know from a letter that he wrote to his friend Jan Matuszyński. Jan was shortly to join the insurgent forces, now led by Prince Adam Czartoryski (the uprising was to continue until September 1831), but Chopin scarcely mentioned this. Instead, his letter began with an account of a fine violinist (Josef Slavík) whose playing had impressed him; he then allowed his concern for the Polish

An eye-witness's record of the
Warsaw uprising, 1831 (Lebrecht)

cause to turn to self-
regard and vacillation:

*I am the most
irresolute creature in
the world ... If it
weren't that I'd
perhaps be a burden
on my father, I'd
return at once. I
curse the day of my
departure, and you'll understand, knowing my situation, that since Tytus left, too many
troubles have fallen on my head all at once. All these dinners, soirées, concerts and
dances which I'm up to the neck in bore me to death. I feel so depressed, dull and gloomy
here. I enjoy these things, but not in such cruel circumstances ... in a drawing room I
pretend to be calm, but on returning home I vent my rage on the piano. I've no one to talk
freely to and must behave charmingly to everyone. There are many people who like me,
paint my picture, fuss over me and try to be nice, but what's the use when I have no peace
of mind — except perhaps when I take out all your letters ... Forgive me for complaining
to you like this, but it seems to take half the weight off my shoulders and calms me
down. I've always shared my feelings with you ... I have a letter from the Saxon court*

to the Vicereine at Milan. But how am I to make the journey? My parents tell me to do as I please, but I don't like to. Shall I go to Paris? People here advise me to wait. Shall I return home? Or stay here? Or kill myself? Or stop writing to you? Do tell me what to do. Ask those who influence me, send me their advice and I'll follow it. I'll stay here all next month, so write before you set out for the north-east {to join the Polish forces}.

This letter addressed to a compatriot about to risk his life hardly does him credit. But his apparent small concern over his friend and his country may reflect a fear of his letters being censored by the Austrian authorities, who, on finding pro-revolutionary sentiments, could expel him from Vienna as an agitator. Even so, it is hard to escape the conclusion that his patriotism was only skin deep. Although he used handkerchiefs embroidered with Polish emblems and enjoyed the company of expatriate countrymen, it never made him risk his career. Again, he only considered his own viewpoint when he wrote to Elsner at the end of January 1831, 'The events in Warsaw have changed my situation here for the worse, to the same extent as they might have improved my chances in Paris.' Thus, he welcomed the flattering advice of new Viennese friends, the physician Johann Malfatti and his Polish wife, which was that an artist such as he belonged to the whole world and should remain above national issues.

Chopin's letter to Matuszyński ends with a description of his daily life:

I live on the fourth floor in what is really the most beautiful street, so high up that I have to lean right out of the window to see what's happening down below. Young

Hummel {Karl, the young son of the musician} has drawn a picture of my room (you will see it in my new album when I return to the bosom of my family); it's large and neat, with three windows. My bed is opposite the windows; on the right is my marvellous piano {on loan from the maker, Graff} and on the left a sofa. There are mirrors between the windows and in the centre a fine big mahogany round table. A polished parquet floor. Very quiet. Monsieur is not at home after dinner, so I can fly to you all in my thoughts. In the morning my insufferably stupid servant wakes me, I get up, my coffee is served, I sit down to play and often have to drink my coffee cold. Then at around nine my German teacher comes; after the lesson I usually play and then Hummel draws my portrait and Nidecki {a pianist friend} practises my concerto – at least that's what's happened lately. I stay in my dressing gown until noon, when Leidenfrost, a good little German chap who works at the prison, turns up and if it's fine we go for a walk on the city ramparts. Then it's time for me to go lunch if I'm invited out, if not we both go to 'The Bohemian Cook', a café where all the university students eat. After lunch one drinks coffee at the finest coffee-house, such is the fashion here. Then I pay my calls, come home at dusk, tidy my hair, put on my evening shoes and go off to a party. About ten or eleven, sometimes twelve but never later, I come home, play the piano, have a good cry, read, look at things, have a laugh, get into bed, blow out my candle and always dream about you all.

There is no mention here of his friend Romuald Hube, seven years older and one of the group with whom he had previously travelled to Vienna; however, Hube briefly became his flatmate on returning from Italy and finding himself unable to enter Poland. He was later to remember Chopin practising the piano, frequently working at subtle details of touch and texture, as well as improvising.

Thus Chopin accustomed himself to Viennese life. The Malfattis entertained him often and kept an eye on his health, thinking him underweight and feeding him up with Polish dishes that were intended to make him feel at home. Other households, sometimes with Polish links, also opened their doors to him, and on the musical side he continued to seek enjoyable new experiences, not least in his visits to the opera house.

Even so, he soon began to express a disillusion with Viennese life and occasionally made scornful remarks about everything German or Austrian. In his diary, he wrote bitterly: 'Everything makes me sigh and long for home, for those lovely times that I failed fully to appreciate ... The people here mean nothing to me; they're kind, but only from habit, not kindness; all they do is flat, mediocre, too ordered, and that dismays me.' He was also displeased at the success of another pianist, Sigismond Thalberg, a couple of years younger than he and boasting an aristocratic descent and an impeccable keyboard technique: 'He plays remarkably, but not to my liking ... the ladies like him ... he takes tenths like I do octaves and wears diamond shirt-studs.' Equally tasteless, he thought, was the local passion for waltzes and little else: 'It all goes to show how the Viennese public's taste has declined.' Some of this was surely sour grapes, as he stayed in the city without making any artistic mark.

However, it was during this time that he wrote his own splendid Waltz in E♭ major, Opus 18, and the more sombre but equally fine Waltz in A minor, Opus 34 No.2. Both pieces are civilized music, but the angry Scherzo in B minor, also composed at this time, may reflect his frustrations, just as its quieter central section, based on a Polish lullaby, may suggest homesickness. So may his two Polish songs to poems by Stefan Witwicki. Similarly, his splendidly dramatic First Ballade, in G minor, conceived in May–June 1831, may be the outcome of feelings which he could only express in musical terms.

Chopin's problem was that Vienna was rich in music and musicians, and he was just another gifted artist among many. Yet he still stayed on in the city. Finally, on 4 April, he got the opportunity to play his E minor Concerto at an afternoon concert in the Redoutensaal, but did so only as a minor contributor to the programme and playing the work only as a piano solo. A few weeks later, on 11 June, he repeated this performance, and this time the press did at least notice it, calling him 'a sincere worshipper of true art', but he wrote in his diary that he no longer cared if the concert took place.

By now, he had applied for a visa to travel to Paris. Unfortunately, the application had to be made to the Russian embassy, where he was already slightly under suspicion for his links with Polish nationalists, while Paris, with her history of revolution, was politically suspect. On a friend's advice, he therefore told the embassy officials that he intended to travel 'to London, via Paris', which is how his passport was endorsed when he eventually received it back. The whole process took some time, firstly because the Austrian authorities mislaid the passport, and secondly because a cholera epidemic in Vienna made it necessary for Chopin to obtain a health certificate before leaving.

In the meantime, he told his parents in a letter dated 16 July:

I don't lack anything, except maybe a bit more life and spirit: I feel weary, and then sometimes as happy as at home. When I'm sad I usually go to Mrs Szaszek's, where I always find some Polish ladies whose sincere, comforting words inevitably cheer me so much that I start mimicking Austrian generals. This is my new act: you haven't yet seen it, but people who do always fall about laughing.

He asked his father to sell the diamond ring that the Russian emperor had given him, saying, 'I'm already costing you quite enough,' but in the meantime obtained an advance of cash from a Viennese bank. As for his memories of Konstancja Gladkowska, he wrote in his diary, 'Sometimes I think I no longer love her, yet I can't get her out of my head.'

When the passport and Paris visa finally arrived, he and an older friend, Alfons Kumelski, left Vienna on 20 July, travelling first to Salzburg, where they visited Mozart's birthplace in the Getreidegasse. They then went on to Munich, where Chopin expected to be able to collect a bank draft from his father. However, this was delayed, and so he stayed for a month, during which time he got to know some of the city's musicians. Thanks to their interest, a concert was arranged for 28 August at which he played his E minor Concerto and his Fantasia on Polish Airs with orchestra in the hall of the city's Philharmonic Society, and the local musical journal, *Flora*, praised both works as well as their composer's 'charming delicacy of execution'.

When the money from Nicolas arrived in Munich, Chopin travelled on to Stuttgart – alone, since Kumelski stayed in the Bavarian capital. As always, he had enjoyed congenial company; but now, on his own, he was troubled by fears as to the safety of his family and friends in Warsaw, from whom he had received little news, and now he learned that the Russians were about to recapture the city from the insurgent Polish forces. On 8 September, he learned that Warsaw had fallen to Russian troops under the notoriously brutal General Pashkievitch, and scribbled in his diary:

The suburbs are destroyed, burned ... O Jaś! {Jan Matuszyński} Wiluś {Wilhelm Kolberg} has probably died on the ramparts! I can see Marceli {Woyciechowski} in chains! Sowiński {a Polish general}, that kind old man, in the hands of those scoundrels! O God, You exist and yet You

Chopin, by Eikhorn (Lebrecht)

do not punish! Have You not seen enough Russian crimes, or maybe You are Russian Yourself! My poor father, perhaps you have nothing left to buy bread for my mother! Maybe my sisters have succumbed to the fury of the Russian mob! Pashkievitch, that Mohilev cur, has stormed the capital of the first European kings! Russia rules the world! O father, so this is your reward in old age! ... They have burned the city! O, why could I not have killed at least one Russian! O, Tytus, Tytus ... What is happening to her {Konstancja}, where is she, unfortunate creature, perhaps in Russian hands? ... Perhaps I have no mother any more ... I am inactive, sitting empty-handed, just sighing and suffering at the piano, despairing ... God, God, move the earth, may it swallow up the people of this century, may the cruellest tortures fall upon the French, who would not help us!

It is often said that the 'Revolutionary' Study in C minor, Opus 10 No.12, was composed in Stuttgart at this time and in response to these events. While this remains unproven, the piece fits the facts in that it is both wild and thrilling: here is a case of poetic truth at least, embodying what Chopin meant by 'suffering at the piano'. Adam Zamoyski has suggested that 'the sense of loss sustained on that night in Stuttgart never left him. It came to embrace everything – home, country, family, friends, love and youth – and remained the fundamental inspiration for his music. As he had promised Konstancja, he would 'heal the wounds of the present with memories of the past'.

Paris

Chopin's journey from Stuttgart to Paris was made in a series of public coaches and the trip took nearly two weeks. But on reaching France in mid-September he at once felt more at home than in Germany, not least because he spoke the language quite well, although with an accent. Furthermore, most French people sympathized with the Polish national cause.

After a night in an inn, he soon found a lodging, up five flights of stairs at 27 Boulevard Poissonnière: the room, attractively furnished in mahogany, had a balcony that looked out on the city's 'finest districts' (as he wrote) including the neo-Grecian Panthéon and the hill of Montmartre with its great domed church of Sacré-Coeur. All this was exciting, and he was soon exploring the city, not least because he needed to hire a piano and then to find what Paris could offer him. His first impressions were confusing but mainly good: here was the biggest and newest-looking city that he had seen, which even had some gas lighting on its elegant boulevards. This was the place which Goethe had called 'a city where all the best of the realms of nature and world art are open to daily contemplation, a world city where crossing every bridge or square recalls a great past and where a piece of history has unfolded at every street corner'. Here, too, official buildings bore the proud revolutionary inscription, 'Liberty, equality, fraternity or death', words to strike terror into the upholders of the old order in Eastern Europe. In fact, the French Revolution of 1789 had been only the first of several political upheavals; Napoleon Bonaparte had become Emperor in 1804 and then, after conquering much of Europe, suffered defeat at Waterloo in 1815. The Bourbon kings returned until 1830, when another coup brought the Duke of Orléans' son Louis-Philippe to the throne. A moderate ruler at first, his régime was to become harsher as it was threatened by radical forces, and in 1848 another coup was to bring about his abdication. In the meantime, France had seen the rise of a new way of thought, in which individuals might be placed above institutions, and was a haven for revolutionaries from other countries such as Italy and Poland.

In this political climate, a new generation of artists sought freedom and self-expression in ways that had hitherto remained unexplored. In music, their work had been most obviously announced by the first performance, in 1830, of Hector Berlioz's *Symphonie fantastique*, a vividly programmatic portrayal of the passions of a young artist who, desperately in love, has taken opium; while leading figures in the other arts included the dramatist Victor Hugo, the poet Alfred de Musset, the novelist Honoré de Balzac and the painter Eugène Delacroix. Paris boasted excellent orchestras and more than one fine opera house, and was second to none in its display of superb singers, among whom were the sopranos Maria Garcia Malibran and Giuditta Pasta.

Thus Paris thrilled Chopin, and he also felt more free to relax since he had heard that his parents were safe. Before long he gave his friend Kumelski a lively account of the city:

You find here the greatest splendour, the greatest filth, the greatest virtue and the greatest vice: at every step you see posters advertising cures for venereal disease ... One disappears in this swarming confusion and in one way it's very convenient, no one asks

Evening entertainments in Paris, by A Provost (AKG)

how you live ... One day you can eat the biggest dinner for 32 sous in a gaslit restaurant full of mirrors and gilt, and then next day you lunch at a place where you get just enough to feed a bird and pay three times as much; it happened to me at first ... And so many kindly young ladies: they go for the men, and there are plenty of strong lads about. I regret that the souvenir of Teresa (despite the efforts of Benedict who thinks my misfortune trifling) hasn't allowed me to taste the forbidden fruit ... I've got to know a few lady singers, and such ladies here, even more than Tyroleans, would willingly join in duets.

left and right *Delfina Potocka (Lebrecht)*

What was 'the memory of Teresa', that prevented him from indulging in flirtations and casual affairs? According to most biographers, this remark tells us that he had recently contracted a sexually transmitted disease, perhaps in Kumelski's company; but if this was indeed a problem (in which case Benedict was probably a doctor), he seems little troubled by it and there is no further evidence. His biographer George Marek adds the plausible suggestion that, although Chopin thought himself to be infected, doubtless with gonorrhoea, that may not have been the case.

He knew no one in Paris, but did not have to wait long before making friends. Some were Polish, like Countess Kisseliev, a member of the aristocratic Potocki family now separated from her Russian husband. There were also the Komars, whose daughter Delfina Potocka was now separated from her husband Mieczyslaw Potocki after an unhappy marriage and led an independent life, enjoying a princely allowance. Both these ladies received guests, and Chopin was soon among them, telling Kumelski, 'Yesterday I dined with Mme Potocka ... I am gradually acquiring the entrée to society, though I have only a ducat in my pocket.' Another Polish host was Count Ludwik Plater, who had represented the insurgent government on diplomatic missions; with his brother Vladislav, he edited a nationalist newspaper called *Le Polonais*.

On the musical side, Chopin profited most from a letter of introduction to the operatic composer and singing teacher Ferdinando Paer, given him by Johann Malfatti. Italian by birth but long resident in Paris, Paer at once proved a good friend and helped Chopin obtain permission to live in the city 'until further notice, to practise his art'. He also introduced him to leading musicians, including Rossini, the greatest operatic composer of the time. It was not long before Chopin was a

Chopin was introduced to Rossini in Paris and was a great admirer of the composer's work (AKG)

Rossini.

regular attender of opera performances, and his enthusiasm bubbled over in a letter of 12 December to Tytus Woyciechowski:

Never have I heard The Barber [of Seville} *as last week, with Lablache, Rubini and Malibran (Garcia), nor* Otello *as with Rubini, Pasta and Lablache, or, again,* Italiana in Algeri *as with Rubini, Lablache and Mme Raimbeaux. Now, if ever, I have everything in Paris. You cannot conceive what Lablache is like! They say that Pasta has gone off, but I never saw anything more sublime. Malibran impresses you merely by her marvellous voice, but no one* sings *like her. Miraculous! Marvellous! … If ever magnificence was seen in a theatre, I doubt whether it reached the level of splendour shown in* Robert le Diable, *the very latest five-act opera of Meyerbeer, who wrote* Il Crociato {in Egitto}. *It is a masterpiece of the modern school.*

Given Chopin's passion for opera and operatic singers, it may seem surprising that he never tried his hand at writing for the theatre, especially as his old teacher Elsner longed for him to do so. This we know from a letter to Chopin from his sister Ludwika (usually referred to as Louise), dated 27 November 1831:

Mr Elsner doesn't wish to see you merely as a concert-giver, a piano composer and famous performer – that's the easy way and far less important than writing operas. He wants to see you in the role for which Nature intended and fitted you. Your place must be with Rossini, Mozart, etc. Your genius should not cling to the piano and concert-giving: operas must bring you immortality.

Later, in a letter dated 14 September 1834, Elsner himself wrote to Chopin:

> *I would like to live to see an opera of your composition, which would not only increase your fame but benefit the art of music in general ... I recognize in addition to your genius the nature of your gifts ... only an opera can show your talent in a true light and win for it eternal life.*

But as far as we know, Chopin never seriously considered stepping outside the role that he had set himself, that of a pianist and a composer for the piano. Another introduction from Paer was to the eminent pianist Friedrich Kalkbrenner, who also taught at the Conservatoire. Chopin had already heard outstanding pianists in Paris, but he was bowled over by this brilliant man, now in his early forties, whose style was polished and who cultivated (and taught) a keyboard technique in which the fingers were strong and independent and the body relatively still. He told Tytus:

> *Herz, Liszt, Hiller and the rest – they're all nobodies compared with Kalkbrenner. I declare that I've played as well as Herz, but I long to play like Kalkbrenner. If Paganini is perfection itself, Kalkbrenner is his equal but in quite a different field. It is impossible to describe his calm, his enchanting touch, his incomparable evenness and the mastery which he reveals in every note – he's a giant who tramples underfoot the Herzes, Czernys and, of course, me!*

Invited to play by Kalkbrenner, Chopin 'put aside all conceit' and played his E minor Concerto, and Kalkbrenner pleased him by saying that he played like a pupil

Place Vendôme, Paris - to become Chopin's home (AKG)

of Field. 'From then on we've seen each other daily, either at his house or mine,' Chopin told Tytus, 'and now that he's got to know me well he proposes that I should become his pupil for three years and that he will make of me something very, very ... !'

Clearly he was tempted by Kalkbrenner's offer, but when he told his family, both they and Elsner opposed the idea. 'It is very flattering that Mr Kalkbrenner has shown such friendship,' his father wrote,

but, my dear boy, I cannot imagine how, with the talent that he claims to find in you, he should think it necessary for you to spend three years under his tuition in order to make an artist out of you and give you a solid foundation {a phrase that Kalkbrenner must have used} – I don't understand this last expression ... I should be glad if you would postpone your decision until you have weighed the matter carefully, listened to advice and thought it over.

Elsner also wrote to advise that Kalkbrenner could serve Chopin better as a friend than as a teacher and that he should not risk losing his individuality: 'No one man ... should be taken as the unsurpassably perfect model.' Finally Chopin came round to this view, not least because he had to earn a living, and told Kalkbrenner of his decision, writing to Tytus: 'I know how much I still have to learn, but I don't just wish to imitate him and three years is too long ... Many people advise me against it, judging that I play as well as he does ... notwithstanding all this business, I am giving a concert on 25 December: you should know that I already have an enormous reputation among the artists.' He and Kalkbrenner remained on excellent terms, and he presented the older man with the dedication of his E minor Concerto. In the concert mentioned above (which, for various reasons, was postponed until 26 February) they joined in a performance of Kalkbrenner's Grand Polonaise with Introduction and March for six pianos; the other works included Chopin's 'Là ci darem' Variations and the F minor Concerto played as a piano solo.

The event took place in the Salle Pleyel, which Chopin used free of charge, thanks to Kalkbrenner, who was a partner in Pleyel's piano firm; it was attended by many leading musicians, including Liszt and Mendelssohn, and at once placed Chopin among Paris's leading pianists. A few days later, the influential critic of the *Revue musicale*, François Joseph Fétis, wrote:

> *Piano music is generally written in certain conventional forms that may be thought basic and which have been continually reproduced for over thirty years. It is one of the defects of this type of music, and our most skilful artists have not succeeded in freeing their works from it. But here is a young man who, surrendering himself to his natural impressions and taking no model, has found, if not a total renewal of piano music, at least something of what we have long vainly sought, namely an abundance of original ideas of a kind found nowhere else ... I find in M. Chopin's inspirations the signs of a renewal of forms which may henceforth exercise considerable influence upon this branch of the art.*

Liszt now became a friend, and Chopin's admiration for the Hungarian pianist's spectacular skill was reflected in the dedication 'to his friend, F. Liszt' of the Twelve Studies, Opus 10, completed in August 1832 and published a year later in Leipzig,

The Salle Pleyel, Rue Rochechouart, Paris: venue for a number of Chopin's recitals (Lebrecht)

A portrait of the composer by his great friend, Franz Liszt (Lebrecht)

Paris and London (his principal French publisher was from now on Maurice Schlesinger). This near-simultaneous appearance of his work in three European cities marked how far his career had moved forward since his disappointment with Haslinger in Vienna a year before.

So did the review of his 'Là ci darem' Variations by Robert Schumann, who discovered the music in Leipzig in 1831, ending with the words, 'Hats off, gentlemen, a genius!' Chopin himself was flattered, but also amused by Schumann's relating the work to scenes in Mozart's *Don Giovanni*, telling Tytus: 'As for the fifth bar of the Adagio, he sees Don Juan kissing Zerlina on the D flat! Plater was wondering yesterday just what part of her anatomy her D flat might be, etc! I could die laughing at this German's imagination.' But Schumann, too, became a friend; he persuaded his future wife, Clara Wieck, to perform the Variations in Germany and was eventually rewarded with the dedication of Chopin's Second Ballade in 1839.

In May 1832, Chopin took part in a charity concert held in the hall of the Paris Conservatoire. Here, at last, he could allow a French audience to hear his F minor Concerto with an orchestra, but only the first movement was played and he must have been disappointed when the *Revue musicale* declared that his playing was sometimes too soft and even inaudible. Since this was not the first time that this had been said of him, he probably now came to feel that his keyboard style was unsuited to large halls. He was not a keyboard lion like Liszt: his strength lay in subtlety more than spectacle, and he told Liszt ruefully, 'I'm unsuited to concert-giving; the crowd intimidates me and I feel stifled by its eager breath, paralysed by its curious stare, silenced by its alien faces – while you're made for it, for when you can't captivate your audience, you can at least knock them senseless!'

Chopin dedicated his Polonaise in B major to Clara Wieck: 'the only woman in Germany who can play my music' (Lebrecht)

The Teacher

During Chopin's first months in Paris, his father continued to send him money. He also profited from his concert in February, for the smallish Salle Pleyel had cost him nothing and ticket sales brought him over a thousand francs. Immediately after that occasion, too, the publisher Scheslinger had called on him and offered to print all the new music he could offer, paying for the two concertos and much else.

Very soon, however, he found that he desired a lifestyle that only a substantial income could support. He acquired expensive tastes, not least in clothes, although, as he reached manhood, his appearance could not aspire to the Byronic look that was then fashionable, for he was unusually small, and weighed only about a hundred pounds. His hair was light brown, silky yet thick, his forehead high, his eyes blue-grey, his nose (which embarrassed him) large and aquiline, and his hands pale, thin and strong. He walked with short steps, yet quickly and gracefully, and his voice was soft. Clothes meant much to him, and he liked them both fashionable and immaculate, wearing specially made gloves, silk shirts and velvet waistcoats, to say nothing of perfume from Chardin, shoes from Rapp and hats from Feydeau. The tailor Dautremont normally charged sixty francs for making a frock-coat, but the one Chopin ordered from him, which had gold buttons, cost a hundred and forty.

This was the Chopin of whom Liszt was later to write: 'His bearing had so much distinction and his manners such a mark of good breeding that one naturally treated him as a prince.' Chopin himself, in a letter of January 1833 to his friend Dominic Dziewanowski, had this to say, mixing pride with a characteristic practicality:

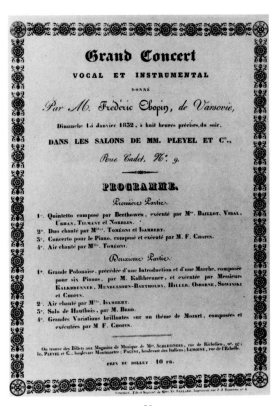

The programme for Chopin's first concert in Paris, 15 January 1832, at the Salle Pleyel (Lebrecht)

I have found my way into the very best society, having my place alongside ambassadors, princes, ministers: I don't know by what miracle this came about, for I have not pushed myself forward. But today all this sort of thing is indispensable to me, for these circles are supposed to be the fountainhead of good taste. You immediately have more talent if you've been heard at the English or Austrian embassies, you at at once play better if Princess Vaudemont has patronized you … I enjoy the friendship and esteem of other musicians … men of the highest reputation dedicate their works to me before I dedicate mine to them … Pupils of the Conservatoire, of Moscheles, Herz, Kalkbrenner – in fact complete artists – have lessons from me and set my name next to Field's, and indeed, if I were a bigger fool than I am, I might think I'd reached the peak of my career. However, I see how far I have still to go, and realize it all the more from mixing intimately with the best artists and observing how far each of them falls short of perfection.

But I feel ashamed of having written so much nonsense. I've boasted like a child or someone with an uneasy conscience, who defends himself before being attacked. I would cross it all out, but haven't time to write another letter. Besides, you've perhaps not forgotten what I'm really like: so remember then that I'm just as I used to be, except that I have one sideburn only, the other simply won't grow.

I have five lessons to give today. You will imagine that I'm making a fortune, but my cabriolet and white gloves cost more than that, and without them I should not have bon ton … I'm a revolutionary myself so I care nothing for money, only for friendship, which I beg you to give me.

'I have five lessons to give today': the phrase is significant. Within his first year in Paris he had found a vocation that would earn him a good, steady living, as a teacher of wealthy piano pupils. His first seems to have been the Countess Pauline Plater, to whom he dedicated the Four Mazurkas, Opus 6, first published in December 1832. But his real entrée to this new profession of fashionable teacher to the aristocracy and the rich appears to have come through Prince Walenty Radziwill, the younger brother of the Prince Radziwill to whom he had dedicated his early Piano Trio and C major Polonaise for cello and piano. Walenty introduced him to the immensely rich and influential Rothschild family, whose social and artistic approval gained him the entrée to great houses; and there, in turn, he found himself in demand. Reading the names of some of his pupils, more famous for their families than for their talent, and mostly female, it is easy to think him more interested in money and social standing than musical ability. But he did not take beginners, and some performers also consulted him: one of them, Wilhelm von Lenz, was older than he and came with a recommendation from Liszt. A boy pupil, Karl Filtsch, was exceptionally gifted: sadly, he died of tuberculosis at fifteen.

As he became established as a teacher, Chopin moved from his first lodging in the Boulevard Poissonnière, first to a furnished flat at 4 Cité Bergère and then to a handsome apartment at 38 Rue de la Chaussée d'Antin. There he employed a manservant and lived the lifestyle of a gentleman, but he could afford it. In fact, his standard fee for a lesson was twenty francs, say fifty pounds or seventy-five dollars today, and he gave five or more daily; one observer, Carl Hallé, reported that he gave up to nine, but that must have been unusual. Whatever the case, there must have been money to spare: at this time, a cab fare was about one franc and a good opera seat cost around ten.

On a teaching day, Chopin began work at eight in the morning, appearing (said one student) like the complete *seigneur*, 'graceful, elegant, impeccably dressed in a jacket of pale violet or blue or hazel buttoned to his chin, his feet small and narrow, always finely shod in shoes of bright leather which shone like a mirror'. We might wonder how anyone dared risk affronting him with the mention of money, did we not know from contemporary accounts of his way of collecting fees. Somehow his pupils were given to understand that, while he was too fastidious for money to be mentioned, at some stage in a lesson he would go to gaze from his window, during which time an envelope with the fee should be left on his mantelpiece; he was never seen to glance in that direction, but by the time the next pupil entered the envelope had gone.

Accounts of Chopin's teaching vary, but all agree in calling it skilful and conscientious. He was mostly patient, but could lose his composure in the face of incompetence or incomprehension and fling a score across the room or break a pencil; on one occasion he even broke a chair. Yet when someone pleased him he could come out with a remark like 'You're an angel'. His chief aim was the production of what is sometimes called 'a singing tone', achieved by skilful touch and the use of the sustaining pedal (which affects sonority as well as allowing strings to sound after keys are released). If a pupil made a harsh sound, he would sometimes ask sarcastically, 'What's this – a barking dog?' Instead of talking of 'striking' the keys, he would say 'let your hands fall'. One pupil, Friederike Müller, wrote:

His playing was always noble and beautiful, his tone always sang whether in full forte *or the softest* piano. *He took infinite pains to teach a pupil this* legato, *cantabile manner of playing. 'He (or she) doesn't know how to link two notes' was his severest censure. He also demanded adherence to the strictest rhythm and hated all lingering and dragging, misplaced* rubatos *and exaggerated* ritardandos. *'Please be seated!', he would say when this happened, with gentle mockery. Indeed, despite the natural flexibility of his own playing, he liked to submit his more self-indulgent pupils to the strict discipline of a metronome.*

His preferred instrument was a Pleyel, and in time he acquired two of these pianos, one a grand and one upright; he liked them, as Liszt later wrote, 'on account of their silvery and somewhat veiled sound and lightish touch'. Seated at one of these two instruments, usually the upright (in his bedroom but usable with the door open), he could demonstrate what he wanted from his pupils. Of course, that did not always solve their technical and interpretative problems: one of them remembered that once, when Chopin played a passage and asked her to perform it in the same way, she felt that it was like a lightning flash making the same request of a damp match.

However artistic a pupil was, Chopin still placed technique first, as a *sine qua non* of quality playing. Generally his method was orthodox, although he did have some special fingerings and in the matter of scale-playing he took C major last, as the most difficult to play because of the difficulty of passing the thumb under when playing only white notes. He sometimes devised exercises intended to achieve the greatest evenness of touch combined with the greatest fluency. It was always important to him that a pianist's elbows should be level with the white keys (thus a lowish seat was needed) and that a basic 'five fingers covering five notes' position should be the norm. Yet for all this emphasis on fundamentals, he discouraged long hours of practice, advising three hours daily as the maximum advisable. It was grace

*Franz Liszt (1811–1886), a close
friend of Chopin's (AKG)*

and ease that he sought to impart, and he would often say '*facilement, facilement*' as he heard a pupil striving to produce a rounded tone and a fine melodic line. Sometimes he urged his pupils to attend the opera and learn how Italian singers shaped their melodies.

Of course, he did not teach only his own music. Friederike Müller, who spent three years with him, remembered his playing to her, unexpectedly and from memory, no less than fourteen preludes and fugues from Bach's *The Well-Tempered Clavier*, which he considered indispensable from the point of view of finger technique, adding, 'This, one never forgets.' Other standbys of his method, far removed from the 'romantic' style to which most of his pupils aspired, were books of studies by Clementi (his *Gradus ad Parnassum*) and Cramer. He also gave his pupils music by Handel, Scarlatti, Hummel and Mozart; less often he would ask them to study music by Field, Weber, Moscheles and Beethoven. To a British lady pupil who took along Beethoven's Sonata in A♭ major, Opus 26, he was revelatory as to the production of a singing (*cantabile*) touch in the lyrical variations of the first movement, showed her how the noble, minor-mode Funeral March should be 'grand, orchestral, powerfully dramatic' and yet refined, and indicated, by playing it himself, what the finale needed, 'faultless precision and extraordinary delicacy – not a single note lost, and with marvellous phrasing and alternations of light and shade'.

But when he did teach his own music, it was especially illuminating. The lady quoted above (her name is unknown because she wished to remain anonymous when writing to a biographer in 1903) had this to say:

This I found fascinating in the highest degree, but very difficult. He would sit patiently while I tried to thread my way through mazes of intricate and unaccustomed modulations, which I could never have understood had he not invariably played to me each composition – nocturne, prelude, impromptu, whatever it was – letting me hear the framework (if I may so express it) around which these beautiful and strange harmonies were grouped, and in addition showing me the special fingering, on which so much depended, and about which he was very strict.

He spoke very little during the lessons. If I was at a loss to understand a passage, he played it slowly to me. I often wondered at his patience, for it must have been torture to listen to my bungling, but he never uttered an impatient word. Sometimes he went to the other piano and murmured an exquisite impromptu accompaniment.

For whatever reason, he did not accept every prospective pupil. He disliked people who were unkempt in their dress or obstinate in their ways. For example, one proud mother, a relative of the poet Alfred de Musset, wrote to him: 'My daughter returned yesterday desperate and discouraged, having studied all the summer in the hope that you would welcome her devotion, only to receive a rigorous and implacable refusal.' Later, she tried again: 'I harbour a tiny hope that perhaps you would now be willing to add my daughter to the list of your pupils ... If this note remains unanswered, I will understand that you wish to spare me the pain of a refusal.' The note did remain unanswered. Though we do not know why he refused this particular girl, clearly Chopin could indeed be implacable, and by this time he had long been free of the financial necessity to accept everyone. Even so, his career as a piano teacher was a full-time affair. It has been calculated that he taught well over a hundred pupils in the fifteen years or so that he practised as a teacher. Indeed, after he had been teaching for something over a year, his father urged him (in a letter dated 7 December 1833) not to overwork:

I see by your letter that you are extremely busy. At your age occupation is necessary and leisure often harmful. But do take care lest the work fatigue you. You must think of your health, and surely your work is not routine. I won't reproach you for frequenting high society, I fear only that your evenings last too late. You need rest.

New Friends and Travels

The picture that we now have of Chopin is of a successful man who enjoyed his work and the elegant lifestyle that it brought him. Yet we know little about his inner life. Did he have no lovers in Paris, and no intimate friends to compare with those of earlier years? What of his social life?

Unfortunately, we do not know as much as we should like, and, moreover, one source of information is suspect. The reason lies primarily in Chopin's natural reserve: one specialist in his music, Alan Walker, has gone so far as to say that he 'lost no opportunity of revealing nothing about himself'. While he applied this remark chiefly to Chopin the composer, it also fits Chopin the man, at least from this time onwards, for he became more reticent as he matured. When Konstancja Gladkowska married in 1831, he informed Tytus, but so casually that he appeared to have lost interest. However, he also confessed to him in letters:

I wish you were here, I'm so miserable with nobody to confide in ... Outwardly I'm cheerful, especially among my own people (meaning Poles), but inside I'm tortured by all sorts of forebodings, fears, dreams or sleeplessness, desire and indifference, the impulse to live and the wish to die ... Everything seems sour, bitter, salty – a dreadful mixture of feelings troubles my mind ... and when it comes to my emotions, I'm always out of step with others.

But Tytus was far away, and before long he married and brought up his family in

Poland, outliving Chopin by thirty years. So Chopin turned inwards upon himself, except, of course, in his music, which seems to have expressed his most passionate feelings. Several people noticed this aspect of his personality, and Liszt was later to write of him, perceptively: 'He was prepared to give anything, but never himself. Good-natured, amiable, easy in all relationships, even-tempered, he barely allowed us to suspect the secret convulsions which agitated him.'

However, we know something of his way of life. By 1833, he was famous, and as George Marek puts it:

> ... *the man one had to, and wanted to, invite for dinner ... If there beckoned a promise of an evening during which he might sit at the piano, the hostess could count on as full a house as if Louis Philippe had scheduled an appearance. The best wine was brought from the cellar, the finest Brussels napery spread on the table. If Chopin came, Hugo or Balzac or de Vigny would not be far behind. The candles shone on those miraculous hands. There was silence. How exquisite, the privilege to be the first to hear that new ballade, even if one did not quite understand it!*

Since Chopin now played only rarely in public, in complete contrast to Liszt, whose long concert tours were legendary, people were only likely to hear him in this kind of situation, nominally private although some hostesses kept virtually open house to their friends on chosen occasions. But he was not one to be put upon or exploited. The French composer Berlioz – whom he liked as a man while having reservations about his music – remembered one occasion when he refused to perform:

Chopin's salon at 12 Place Vendôme, Paris (Lebrecht)

Scarcely had the company had coffee when the host, approaching Chopin, told him that the other guests who had never heard him hoped that he would be so good as to sit down at the piano and play them some little trifle. Chopin excused himself from the first in a way that left no doubt whatever as to his inclination. But when the other insisted in an almost offensive manner, like a man who knows the price and purpose of the dinner he has just given, the artist cut the conversation short by saying in a weak and broken voice and with a fit of coughing, 'Ah, sir, but I have only eaten very little!'

Sometimes Chopin entertained at home, planning the dishes himself and having them served on fine crockery and with antique silver cutlery. A visit to Chopin's home was a rare distinction, particularly after he redecorated his flat, changing the chair covers from red to white silk: 'impractical but ravishing, and red hurts my eyes'. The furniture was of rosewood, and beautiful, and the wallpaper pearl-grey, a colour he considered 'not glaring or common'. In these elegant surroundings, a Louis XV clock and a collection of French porcelain also had their place, as did his Pleyel grand piano. His bedroom also contained his upright piano, the bed being in a curtained-off alcove; here, too, an easy chair bore a tapestry embroidered by his mother, and on a marble table was a silver incense burner. Was Chopin, brought up as a Catholic, devout enough to pray regularly? It seems unlikely, for he was not a churchgoer. His characteristic hypochondria was attested by a well filled medicine cabinet. Throughout the apartment, silk and muslin curtains softened the light, and there were paintings and etchings. He also liked to fill a room with the scent of violets. Frankly, he was now something of a dandy, and one pupil commented, 'He lived like a woman, almost a *cocotte* – a woman of easy virtue.'

For all this physical comfort, it remains doubtful whether Chopin was a happy man, although we need not take too seriously Liszt's remark in a letter of 1834, 'Chopin is all sadness. Furniture is a bit more expensive than he had expected, so now we're in for a whole month of worry and nerves.' And he still received fussy letters from his father, who thought him not yet mature enough to do without parental advice. In April 1833, Nicolas wrote:

> *If you are satisfied, so are we. But I must continue to repeat that until you have put a couple of thousand francs aside, I shall regard you as to be pitied, despite your talent and the flattering compliments you receive. Compliments are so much smoke that won't keep you alive in needy times. May God preserve you from poor health or illness, or else you will be reduced to poverty in a foreign land. I admit such thoughts often trouble me, for I see that you spend as fast as you earn.*

Chopin replied mildly and dutifully, but a few months later Nicolas wrote again:

> *I rejoice to hear you speak of your principles. Yes, dear boy, a young man can easily be led astray if he does not watch himself … At your age you must avoid any kind of impropriety; do not be led into intrigues that might cause much embarrassment … How are things going, my boy? Do you manage to save up a few pennies (I always harp on that!)? Try to accumulate a little reserve: I would advise putting it into things that you can convert back into cash whenever you like.*

Nicolas also worried that his son lived alone. For a while, a doctor friend called Aleksander Hoffmann had moved in, but Hoffmann's pipe-smoking had proved troublesome: 'It worries me very much that you have not a real friend living with you. As you say, the other arrangement did not work, for you can't receive friends in a room full of smoke, especially as you don't smoke yourself. Yet it is miserable to be entirely alone with nobody to talk to'. Nicolas was pleased, therefore, when Jan Matuszyński, now also qualified as a doctor ('I've always liked him, a good lad'), arrived in Paris early in 1834 to take up a teaching post and Chopin took him in as a flatmate.

Clearly, Nicolas had something of Shakespeare's fussy, elderly Polonius about him, and his well-intentioned advice may have been irksome. But his letters do suggest a continuing anxiety that his son might somehow go off the rails. What kind of 'impropriety' or 'intrigue' did he fear? Probably he meant an involvement in a sexual scandal and wondered whether his impressionable son could avoid such a thing in the permissive Parisian social circles in which he moved. But only Chopin knew the answer to that. His own letters show that he was susceptible to feminine charms, but was reluctant to start a serious affair. That there was no whiff of scandal in his life was probably a professional necessity while parents allowed their daughters, as his pupils, to be alone with him in his apartment. He once called on a pianist called Johann Peter Pixis and, finding him out, sat down instead with a young girl 'pupil' (perhaps Pixis' mistress); and when Pixis returned and looked angry and suspicious, Chopin was amused and told Tytus, 'I couldn't hide my joy in thinking that anyone could think me *capable* of such a thing! ... Me, a seducer!' Why not?

Jan Matuszynski: Chopin's doctor, friend and flatmate (Lebrecht)

Probably he found that while he could be attracted to women, he remained more comfortable in male company, avoiding love but enjoying warm friendships. The German pianist Ferdinand Hiller, a year younger than he, became such a friend. 'I think I can say that Chopin loved me, but I was in love with him,' declared Hiller in later years. It was Hiller who introduced Chopin to Vincenzo Bellini, when the Italian composer visited Paris in the autumn of 1833; with the singer Lina Freppa, these three men enjoyed meeting and making music. Other friends at this time included two Poles living in Paris, Julian Fontana and Albert Grzymala, who were henceforth to remain among his intimates for the rest of his life. But there was no woman to play a central part in his life.

Or was there? For all these reasons, as well as others, we must remain suspicious about the affair that some writers believe Chopin had in around 1833 with Delfina Potocka, although it is possible that they had a brief physical relationship. Beautiful and a fine singer and pianist, she lived alone and they were certainly friends: indeed, he dedicated to her his F minor Concerto, when it was published in 1836, and much later, in 1847, his 'Minute' Waltz in D♭ major, Opus 64 No.1. She had several distinguished lovers, and the Polish poet Adam Mickiewicz used mischievously to call her 'the great sinner'. But was Chopin among them? The contemporary evidence is twofold: a letter written after his death by a Pole living in Paris, Jozef Mycielski, and the testimony of Aleksander Hoffmann's widow, who said that her husband remembered Delfina staying overnight in Chopin's apartment. But the first of these witnesses did not know Chopin, and Madame Hoffmann, speaking sixty years after these events, also made the ridiculous claim that her husband had lived with the composer for years and helped with his compositions. The only complete surviving

Vincenzo Bellini and Chopin often met to
make music together (AKG)

A bronze medal of
Julian Fontana by
Oleszczynski, 1843
(Lebrecht)

letter from Delfina to Chopin belongs to 1849 and begins, 'Dear M. Chopin, I do not wish to trouble you with a long letter': this hardly suggests a former lover. Nor does Chopin's calling her 'Mme. D. Potocka' in his private diary. Finally, according to Liszt, Chopin denied to him and others that they had had an affair.

However, in 1945 a Polish woman called Paulina Czernicka announced her discovery of a number of letters from Chopin to Delfina Potocka, claiming to have received them from one of Potocka's descendants. They were of an explicit nature and sometimes obscene, in a way that seems foreign to Chopin's character as we otherwise know it (Liszt declared that he 'winced as much at a coarse thought as he did at a muddy shoe or a speck of dust on his frock coat') and also contained numerous comments on music and musicians which did not ring true. No originals were ever produced, only copies. After her death in 1949, Mme Czernicka's papers were found and examined, and the consensus of opinion is that there is a small authentic part of the correspondence but that most of it was forged. Paulina Czernicka seems to have been both obsessed by Chopin and psychologically disturbed, and her death was a suicide. The case for and against the 'Potocka letters' is discussed at length in the Chopin biographies by Adam Zamoyski and George Marek, and also in Arthur Hedley's volume of his selected correspondence.

Robert Spies' Romantic interpretation of Prelude No. 22 in G minor (Lebrecht)

Maria Wodzińska and George Sand

Chopin had now ceased to mount concerts for himself, finding it uncongenial and no longer needing the money, although he did still occasionally play in public, for example joining in a concert given by Hiller on 15 December 1833 and playing some of Bach's Concerto for Three Pianos with Hiller and Liszt. His self-imposed seclusion, so different from other pianists, led Liszt to the amused remark that 'there was now not so much the school of Chopin as the church of Chopin'. None of this worried him, for his lifestyle suited him well enough.

In the spring of 1834, he accompanied Hiller to Germany to attend the Lower Rhine Festival which Mendelssohn had organized at Aachen. Mendelssohn welcomed them warmly, writing in a letter that 'as a pianist Chopin is now one of the very best: he astonishes one with novelties, like Paganini on the violin, and introduces wonderful things that one would think impossible'. He thought Chopin's playing prone to emotional exaggeration, but admitted that he himself might err in the opposite direction, 'so we complement and teach each other'.

Hiller and Chopin then accompanied Mendelssohn to Düsseldorf, where Hiller wrote of Chopin, 'He had only played a few bars when everyone … began to look at him very differently; they'd never heard anything like it before. In their enthusiasm they begged him to play again and again.' After this, the three musicians boarded a Rhine steamer together, Chopin and Hiller sailing as far as Koblenz. 'I feel like the steam from our boat', Chopin wrote to Hiller's mother, 'feeling half of me wafting to my people at home and the other half coming to greet you in Paris … Ferdinand is well and looks as if he would be nice to eat!'

Back in Paris, his life resumed its pattern. But he found less time to compose, although some of his Twelve Studies, Opus 25, date from this year. He may have been overworking: at any rate, in March 1835 he went down with influenza that turned to bronchitis, and began coughing blood, and his doctor friend Jan Matuszyński recommended that he should leave Paris for the spa town of Enghien. He may have done so, but not until the summer. In the meantime, he organized a charity concert for a Polish cause on 4 April, playing his E minor Concerto with orchestra and joining Liszt in a duo performance on two pianos to end the evening. Later that month, on the 26th, he performed again at the Conservatoire with the same conductor, François Antoine Habeneck, playing his Andante Spianato and Grande Polonaise, a new work that combined his Polonaise in E♭ major (for piano and orchestra) of 1831 with a substantial introductory movement for piano solo.

In August 1835 he set off for the German spa town of Karlsbad, for his parents had written to say they were going there; this was reason enough, but by doing so he was also heeding Jan's advice as to nursing his health. On arriving, he was told that they were still awaited; in fact they had arrived and, on learning that he was already there, hastened to his room to awake him. 'Our joy is indescribable!' he wrote. 'How good God is to us!' After three weeks, he accompanied his parents on part of their journey home. Near the Polish frontier, where all three stayed for some days as the guests of Count Thun-Hohenstein at Tetschen, he bade them a tearful farewell, promising another meeting. It was never to take place.

As he travelled back towards Paris, he stopped at Dresden at the Stadt Gotha Hotel to make contact with some Polish friends. These were the Wodziński family,

A self-portrait by Maria Wodzińska…(Lebrecht)

now resident in Geneva, with whom he had recently been in touch by letter. Their daughter Maria, who had studied with Chopin in Warsaw and was now sixteen, was an attractive girl with a warm personality and during the fortnight that he spent in Dresden their friendship deepened. However, the letter she sent him after he left on 26 September is rather formal, and when she writes, 'I am boring you – your time's too valuable to waste reading my scribblings,' one hardly thinks of a lover, although Maria would naturally have been discreet on paper. Still, both saw this meeting as the beginning of a romance.

Chopin then passed through Leipzig, met Mendelssohn again and also Schumann, the latter at the house of his future father-in-law Friedrich Wieck, playing to the Germans and hearing young Clara Wieck play – 'the only woman in Germany who can play my music', he said. He then went on to Heidelberg, where he fell ill once more; rumours as to his health began to circulate and some people even believed he had died. His parents became anxious, and so did the Wodzińskis. Finally, he got better and reached Paris late in October, where he found himself playing host to Maria Wodzińska's elder brother Antoni, who came to stay and had to be entertained. He became tired, but refused to wear the warm outdoor boots that Dr Matuszyński recommended, and again fell ill in March 1836.

In April he was well enough to give an Easter dinner for friends in his apartment, and he then went to Enghien, where he could build up his strength and also enjoy the hospitality of the wealthy Marquis de Custine, a wealthy man in his forties who led a discreetly homosexual life but was widely liked for his intelligence, wit and generosity. 'Come whenever you like', he told Chopin, who appreciated his company. A contemporary account of a lunch party at the Marquis's 'Florentine villa arranged in the English manner' on the lake of Enghien relates how Chopin's jokes and impersonations kept everyone laughing.

In the meantime, he continued to think of Maria Wodzińska. But although her father Wincenty Wodziński liked Chopin and called on his parents in Warsaw, he did not want his daughter to marry a man in poor health, however famous. Nothing was said, however, and at the end of July 1836 Chopin joined Mme Wodzińska and her daughters at another spa town, Marienbad, staying with them in their hotel for much of August before moving on with them to Dresden. Maria painted his portrait and they took leisurely walks together; and finally on 9 September, the day before his departure, he proposed to her and was accepted. We may wonder why he waited until he was leaving before doing so; possibly he was still unsure of his own feelings. At any rate, Mme Wodzińska insisted that the engagement must remain secret and depended on her husband's agreement, which in turn related to Chopin's health. 'Everything depends on that … you must realize that this is a trial period', she wrote to him on 14 September, urging him to wear warm clothing and go to bed early. Maria had embroidered some slippers for him, a size too large so that he could wear thick socks as well.

The rest of this story may be quickly told. Despite warnings from Mme Wodzińska and his own mother, Chopin failed to change his lifestyle; indeed within a few weeks, he was playing at an all-night Christmas party when 'everyone was so captivated by his playing and the good cheer that no one noticed dawn had broken half an hour before'. During this winter, he again went down with flu, and Maria's letters gradually changed their tone: her mentions of a forthcoming meeting changed from 'May or June at latest' to 'when we next meet' and finally, a sad

...and a watercolour of her suitor, Chopin (Lebrecht)

'Adieu: I trust you will not forget us'. Finally, after a silence, Mme Wodzińska wrote to him without mentioning the engagement or promising a further meeting. He was too shy, or uncertain, to make the determined effort that might have saved his engagement, and although he and the Wodzińskis remained in contact, this romance faded and died. In 1840, Maria became engaged to Count Josef Skarbek and she married him in the following year. The marriage was unhappy and ended in divorce; she then remarried and lived until 1896.

Was it only Chopin's uncertain health that doomed this relationship? Perhaps not: whether or not they ever said so, the Wodzińskis may also have thought his lifestyle too Bohemian, and heard of his closeness to people whose emancipation offended conventional morality, among them Delfina Potocka, the Marquis de Custine, Liszt and his mistress Marie d'Agoult (whom he first met at Chopin's) and the woman novelist George Sand.

Born Lucile-Aurore Dupin in 1804, George Sand had married Baron Dudevant and then separated from him; taking her male pen-name, she then wrote a series of novels that made her famous. A feminist through and through, she wore men's clothes and smoked cigars but remained attractive to men, enjoying a long affair with the poet Alfred de Musset as well as taking other lovers. She had two young children, Maurice and Solange, aged respectively thirteen and eight. Chopin met her for the first time in October 1836 at a party given by Marie d'Agoult. Within a few days she was a guest at this apartment, one of a gathering that also included Liszt and Marie, Mickiewicz and Albert Grzymala. Other meetings followed, and by the end of November, George was one of his circle.

Was he attracted to her at once? Far from it: 'What an unattractive person La

George Sand (Lucile-Aurore Dupin)
in a painting by Leygue (Mansell)

Sand is – is she really a woman?' he asked Hiller. But he liked her company. She in turn was drawn to him, and by April 1837 had invited him, along with Liszt and Marie, to stay at her country house at Nohant. He refused, perhaps partly because he was brooding over Maria Wodzińska and feared that news of such a visit would reach her, partly because he felt too unwell to face a long journey. Marie d'Agoult told George, 'Chopin can't make up his mind – only his cough is dependable.'

His health, from now on, was always to be a matter for concern, and the Marquis de Custine wrote to him in May:

You are ill, and what is worse, your illness may become serious. You've reached the limit in physical and spiritual suffering. When griefs of the heart turn to bodily illness we are lost, and that's what I want to save you from ... It is one's duty to live when one has a fountain of life and poetry like yours: do not waste this treasure, nor treat Providence with contempt ... God Himself will not make good the time you deliberately waste ... Only one thing matters, your health.

Chopin went again to Enghien in June and visited de Custine at his villa, enjoying excursions and playing some of his new music, including his Second Ballade (composed in 1836, but later revised), studies and mazurkas. He also improvised with 'beautiful melody and fiery spirit'. But he was soon back in Paris, taking Jan Matuszyński out for a superb dinner in a restaurant's private room: oysters, game soup, *matelote* (a fish stew) and asparagus, all washed down with champagne. 'With cigars in our teeth we set of for coffee at Tortoni's,' wrote a fellow guest, Jozef Brzowski; though it seems impossible that Chopin, with his diseased chest, could have smoked, once again this kind of evening may have done him harm.

He now decided to accompany his friend Camille Pleyel on a trip to London, reaching the city on 7 July 1837 and at once noting the 'huge urinals', sooty atmosphere (hardly good for his health) and buildings 'as black as a gentleman's bottom!' He enjoyed the opera and visits to Hampton Court, Richmond and Brighton; and at Arundel he saw a Dickensian scene of an election. As for music, he wanted to remain incognito, calling himself 'Mr Fritz', but on a visit with Pleyel to the English piano-maker Henry Broadwood, could not resist sitting down to play and revealing his identity.

Back in Paris, he settled down to a rather dull autumn, and it was probably now that he gathered together all his Wodziński correspondence and tied it in a package on which he wrote the words 'My tragedy'. But he did not forget Maria, instead keeping her in his mind just as he had done Konstancja Gladkowska years before. As for his other friends, Liszt and Marie d'Agoult were in Italy and George Sand was hard at work writing in her country house at Nohant, to the south of Paris. His financial situation may also have been less good than usual: he had spent freely on travel in the previous months and correspondingly neglected his teaching. Now he had to settle down again, but he found it difficult. The music that he wrote at this time also suggests that he was troubled: the laconic Scherzo in B♭ minor is far from playful, and nor is the Funeral March in the same dark key that he later (1839) incorporated into his Second Sonata. At this lonely time, he most enjoyed the company of Polish friends such as Julian Fontana and Albert Grzymala, saying, 'One's greatest solace in a foreign land is to have someone who reminds one of one's homeland every time one looks at him.' And, of course, his French, good though it

'Moja bieda' - My tragedy: Maria Wodzinska's letters to Chopin (Lebrecht)

was, was still not his native language and it was only in Polish that he could fully express himself. On the other hand, the poet Adam Mickiewicz could irk him with their pressure on him to act and speak more forcibly for Polish nationalism instead of 'caressing the nerves of the French aristocracy', as one of them put it. What was he, a true child of Poland, or a Parisian dandy? The question troubled him, but was to remain unanswered: he was Chopin, no more and no less.

He played at court in February 1838, in a concert given by the pianist Alkan (Charles-Valentin Morhange) in March, and, later that month, in Rouen: 'Forward, then, Chopin!' declared the *Gazette musicale*. 'When it shall be asked whether Liszt or Thalberg is the great pianist in Europe, let all reply like those who have heard you, it is Chopin!' Yet after this appearance, it was some time before he next played in public.

In April 1838, George Sand returned briefly to Paris, and she and Chopin were soon in touch: indeed, he played at a party at her house that month. They had both matured since their first meeting and found that they liked each other more and more. One day she sent him a note saying 'I love you. George', which he kept in his wallet. Clearly, she was ready for an affair. But he was reluctant to commit himself. Their mutual friend Grzymala served as an adviser to both parties, and Chopin scribbled him a note begging for a meeting: 'I must see you urgently today, even at midnight or one in the morning.' George then returned to Nohant, and Grzymala wrote to her, apparently telling her of Maria Wodzińska and perhaps advising her not to trifle with Chopin's affections (the letter has not survived and may have been sent without Chopin's knowledge), whereupon George then sent Grzymala an enormously lengthy and emotional reply, which took into account her existing relationship with another lover, her son's tutor Félicien Mallefille:

> *It would never occur to me to doubt the sincerity of your advice, dear friend...Your principles become mine, in saying that one must put one's own happiness last ... This young lady whom he desires, or ought (or thinks he ought) to love, is she the right one to secure his happiness or will she deepen his sufferings and melancholy? ... What I want to know is which of the two of us he must forget or give up if he is to have any peace or happiness ... I don't want to play the part of the evil genius ... For myself I refuse to give way to passion, although a very dangerous fire sometimes smoulders deep in my heart. The thought of my children will strengthen me to crush anything that might part me from them or the lifestyle best for their education, health and well-being ... So my duty is fully mapped out ... Perhaps you had better consider explaining to him my situation with regard to M. {Mallefille} ... I leave you completely free to decide ...*
> *The point I was coming to, the question of {physical} possession: ... I wish to say that he displeased me by one single thing ... he had in his own mind the wrong reasons for abstaining ... He seemed to despise, like a religious prude, the coarser side of human nature, and to blush for temptations he had had, and to fear to soil our love by a further ecstasy. I have always hated this way of regarding the completest embrace of love ... Can there be for lofty natures a purely physical love, and for sincere natures one which is just intellectual? ... He said, I think, that certain actions might spoil our memories ... Tell me, what wretched woman has left him with such impressions of physical love?*

For all these lofty sentiments, George wanted to get Chopin into her bed, and evidently she succeeded. Returning to Paris by the beginning of July, she sent

Two views of Nohant: the house by Maurice Sand (Lebrecht)…

Mallefille on an 'educational tour' with her son, and proceeded to seal her new liaison. After a month, she wrote to the painter Eugène Delacroix of 'the delicious exhaustion of fulfilled love' and later, 'I am beginning to think there are angels disguised as men.' In the meantime, Mallefille, returning to Paris, was furious to discover the situation and created scenes; according to one account, he even physically assaulted Chopin, who was rescued by Grzymala.

Having made her conquest, George now decided to travel with Chopin and her children to spend the winter in a Mediterranean climate. After considering Italy, she settled on Majorca, and despite cautionary advice from Grzymala and other friends, Chopin agreed. He borrowed money, contracted in advance the set of Twenty-Four Preludes on which he was working and prepared to leave Paris. George departed on 18 October, and he arranged to set off a week later. In the meantime he visited the Marquis de Custine, who wrote in a letter to a friend dated 22 October:

You simply can't imagine what Mme Sand has done to him ... Consumption has taken possession of that face, making it a soul without a body ... {He played} a funeral march, which made me burst into tears despite myself. It was the procession taking him to his last resting place; and when I reflected that perhaps I would never see him again on this earth, my heart bled. The unfortunate creature can't see that the woman's love is that of a vampire! He's following her to Spain, where she's preceding him. He will never leave that country. He did not dare tell me where he was going, but only spoke of his need for a good climate and rest. Rest! – with a ghoul as his travelling companion!

… and the garden by Eugene Delacroix (AKG)

Allowing for the Marquis's exaggerated prose, it is still significant that he put his finger on the seriousness of Chopin's physical condition, and even the specific illness, tuberculosis of the lungs, from which he was already suffering. Physically at least, the next decade was to be one of decline, and perhaps Chopin knew it.

A Winter in Majorca

After four nights of coach travel, Chopin met George on 30 October at Perpignan, near the Spanish border, looking, according to her, 'as fresh as a rose and pink as a turnip'. This must be nonsense, suggesting her insensitivity over this man whom she desired, although like many sick people he had his ups and downs, and undoubtedly looked forward to the trip. They went on by sea to Barcelona, waited five days for the weekly boat to Majorca and finally reached Palma on 8 November. Accommodation there proved hard to find, but after a week, with the help of the French consul, the party rented a villa and moved in on the 15th. The next day Chopin wrote to tell Fontana: 'The sky is like turquoise, the sea like lapis lazuli, the hills like emeralds, the air like heaven. In the day, sunshine and everyone goes about in summer clothes; at night there's guitars and hours of songs … In a word, this is the most wonderful life.'

The four travellers went on long walks, which were enjoyable until one day a strong wind on their way home put Chopin down with his usual bronchitis. The weather changed, too, becoming colder and rainy, and the villa was now cold and damp. Now anxious, George called in three doctors, as Chopin told Fontana on 3 December:

One sniffed at what I spat, the second tapped where I spat from and the third sounded me and listened as I spat. The first said I was dead, the second that I am dying, and the third that I'm going to die – and I feel the same as ever. I can't forgive Jas

*The monastery at Valldemosa, by
Bartolomé Ferrá (Lebrecht)*

{Matuszyński} for not telling me what to do in the event of acute bronchitis … Don't tell people I've been ill or they'll make a fantastic tale out of it. {Jan Matuszyński himself was to die of tuberculosis in 1842.}

Undefeated, George installed a stove, and he improved a little, rented a local piano, and started work on his Preludes; Nos. 2 and 4, written at this time, are sombre, with No.2 especially black in mood, but that cannot be said of the vivid No.10 and songful No.21. 'I cough and am covered in poultices, awaiting the spring, or something else,' Chopin told Fontana. Then came another blow: the doctors had diagnosed his illness as tuberculosis, and reported it as they were bound by law to do, and he and George were asked to leave their villa after paying for its disinfection and even for new furniture. Fortunately, George had already found accommodation in the deserted monastery of Valldemosa, in the hills above Palma. Chopin wrote: 'Tomorrow I'm going to that marvellous monastery of Valldemosa to write in the cell of some old monk who may have had more fire in his soul than I, but stifled it, stifled and put it out, for it was vain to him.' When he arrived, he was deeply intrigued.

Next to my bed there's a useless square desk that I can hardly use for writing, on it a leaden candlestick (a luxury here) with a candle, some Bach {musical scores that he had brought with him}, my scrawls, someone else's papers … silence … you can yell … still silence. In a word, I'm writing from a strange place … Nature is kind but the people are rogues, for they never see foreigners and never know what to charge for anything. You get oranges for nothing but they ask a huge sum for a trouser button. But that's

A lithograph of Ary Scheffer's portrait of Chopin, 1845 (AKG)

nothing compared with the poetry that everything here breathes and the colour of these lovely places untainted by men's eyes.

Things were far from ideal. Such local people as there were harboured a deep suspicion of this party of foreigners consisting of a woman in trousers, two children and a sick man who was not her husband, who never attended church; George found herself paying over the odds for food and acquired her own goat to supply milk. They would have been hard put to manage without the help of the French consul, who sent some supplies. But she and Chopin both found time to work, she producing her prose and he his music. The intensely dramatic Scherzo in C# minor was written here, and we may perhaps hear in it an echo of the storms that sometimes buffeted the monastery; we may also hear them in the revised version of the Second Ballade that Chopin now completed, which starts in F major but ends in a disruptive A minor. Composition was made easier for him when a piano, sent by Pleyel but held up by the local customs until duty was paid, finally reached him in January, when the weather also changed for the better; with this stimulus he also completed the C minor Polonaise, Opus 40 No.2, and put the finishing touches to the Preludes, sending them off to Paris for publication.

Now their money was running low, and on 11 February the party left Valldemosa for Palma, travelling nine miles in a cart because no one would hire a better conveyance to a man with Chopin's sickness. Awaiting the steamer for Barcelona, he was again ill, and sharing the voyage with a cargo of pigs made him worse; in Barcelona he coughed blood and the party stayed a week in a hotel. They then went on to Marseilles, where they remained until 22 May, taking in a 'couple of quiet

A sketch of Chopin by George Sand
(Mansell)

weeks' in Genoa before finally travelling on to Nohant and reaching George's home on 2 June. 'He seems to want to stay here as long as possible,' George wrote to a friend the next day, 'but I'll take him at his word only as long as I see that the place really benefits him.'

Indeed, Chopin had taken some steps towards relinquishing his apartment in Paris, or at least subletting it, which suggests that he intended a long stay; as for his furniture, he wanted it temporarily shared by Fontana, Grzymala and Matuszyński. In Nohant, he had his own room, and another smaller one with a piano; George was nearby but each had privacy. She liked to sit writing through much of the night and only get up towards midday, but otherwise they shared their lives. Chopin was now in better health and spirits, thanking Grzymala for forwarding funds and adding that he would love his 'angel' George 'still more if you knew her as I do today'. He was grateful to her for patiently nursing him; but he must also sometimes have wondered whether his recent illnesses could have been avoided and whether he had been right to abandon Paris. He must also have missed his Polish and other friends, to say nothing of such delights as the opera. Was this new way of life fully satisfying? As George herself wrote to a friend, 'Natures like his need to be surrounded by refined civilization.' Furthermore, although he could now live on the income from his compositions, he was no longer his own master.

And what of George? Writing from Valldemosa, she had called Chopin 'an angel of patience, gentleness and goodness', but later she was to write that 'the poor great artist was a detestable patient.' What did he mean to her now? Certainly he was no longer the lover that she had desired; indeed, she told a friend, he was 'too fine, too exquisite, too perfect to live long in his crude and heavy world of earth'. From now

Felix Mendelssohn
(AKG)

on, she would often talk about him, and even to him, in maternal terms, and a letter of 1840 tells him, 'Love your old mother as she does you.' What Chopin's parents made of this relationship is hard to know: they must have recognized it as a love affair, and in their eyes a most unsuitable one, but seem to have accepted George's place in their son's life.

During that summer in Nohant, Chopin took his Funeral March of 1837 and incorporated it into a new work, his Second Sonata. Powerfully dramatic and in the dark key of B♭ minor, the Sonata ends with a short but enigmatic movement that has been likened to 'a pursuit in utter darkness', and 'night winds passing over a newly dug grave'. It is hard to avoid concluding that in this music he was already foreseeing his own death. The work puzzled almost all his contemporaries: Schumann said of its four movements that the composer had here 'bound together four of his maddest children', and Mendelssohn could make nothing of the mysterious finale.

In the meantime, the composer was 'never definitely well nor definitely ill', as George wrote in September: 'When he feels a bit stronger he becomes very cheerful, and when he's melancholy he goes to the piano and composes beautifully.' Another piece from this time was calmer, the exquisite F# major Impromptu, Opus 36.

In October 1839, after a full twelve months' absence from Paris, George and Chopin returned there; she had had a play accepted at the Comédie Française and wished to supervise the production, while he was now almost certainly anxious to return. Fontana, who already acted as his agent in dealings with publishers, found him a new apartment at 5 Rue Tronchet, near the Madeleine. Cheered by the prospect, Chopin also sent him surprisingly detailed instructions as to decorating it, getting his furniture back from his friends and finding him a servant: 'Don't offer him more than 80 [francs per month] ... The rubber mattress on my bed needs repair, if that's not too expensive, if it is, leave it. Have the chairs and things properly beaten and dusted.' Fontana also had to order new clothes for him and have them delivered 'so that I can change as soon as I arrive', and was even given the task of finding other accommodation for George, her son and a couple of her servants. A last instruction was: 'Since you're such a clever chap, see to it that all black thoughts and coughing fits are banned from my new abode, and if you can, wipe out many past episodes.' What were they?

A further thought must be for Fontana himself; three years later this loyal friend was to get into financial straits, but as far as we know Chopin did not help. Soon after that, he left Paris for America and stayed there for eight years before returning. He committed suicide in 1869.

Back in Paris, Chopin soon found pupils again and his life began to resume its former pattern; although the Sand affair had been common knowledge and widely discussed, few people held it against him and the gossip had mainly concerned his health – at one stage, Berlioz had written anxiously to ask if he was still alive.

In fact, he was now entering a calmer period. One biographer, Arthur Hedley, goes so far as to write, 'Chopin's life for the next few years appears to be entirely uneventful.' Late in 1839, he composed the *Trois Nouvelles Etudes* which form a pendant to the two books of Twelve studies, Opuses 10 and 25, and in the following spring he wrote his Ab major Waltz, Opus 42.

The only big works of 1840–1 were the F# minor Polonaise and F minor Fantasia, although there were some smaller pieces such as the beautiful Prelude in C# minor, Opus 45, and the Nocturnes in C minor and F# minor, Opus 48. Every one of these was in a minor key and had elements of sadness or storm: perhaps they reflected his state of mind, but his letters of this time are generally unrevealing.

Spies' visual interpretation of Prelude No. 11
in B major (Lebrecht)

The Last Years

Although they no longer wholly shared their lives, Chopin and George remained close, and he spent each of the summers from 1841 to 1846 at Nohant; in 1844 his sister Louise joined them there. He taught his pupils, moved house again in 1842 to share accommodation with her when George was in Paris (at 9 Place d'Orléans) and continued to enjoy the company of his friends, including his Polish intimates, Delacroix and de Custine, who now found him 'still more perfect and noble ... the perfection of art ... it is not the piano that you play but the soul itself'. His health remained fragile, but he had finally learned to conserve his strength and to avoid his former recurrent winter crises, although he was ill in November 1843 ('he coughs, chokes and spits', Maurice Sand told his mother at Nohant).

None the less, tuberculosis gradually gained its hold. His pupil, Friederike Müller, wrote of him: 'Feeble, pale, coughing a great deal, he often took opium drops with sugar or drank a tincture, rubbed his forehead with eau de cologne, but nevertheless taught with an admirable patience, perseverance and zeal.' He once told her, 'I don't have time to be ill.' When another pupil, playing one of his polonaises, broke a string on his piano and apologized, he replied that, had he himself the strength to play it as it should be played, by the time it was over 'not one string would remain unbroken'. Once he was in tears as his twelve-year-old Hungarian pupil Karl Filtsch played his music. One feels that, as he grew older, he increasingly showed that he had never been a natural Bohemian and that he had inherited from his father a true teacher's method and patience.

Chopin aged thirty-seven in a drawing by Lehmann. His health was inexorably declining (Lebrecht)

He now played rarely in public, but when he did everyone was there – if they could afford the seats. After his concert on 26 April at the Salle Pleyel, the journal *Le Ménestrel* declared that 'heart and genius alone' spoke in his art and the poet Heine called him 'the Raphael of the piano'. He netted over six thousand francs from this event, and another five thousand from another concert on 21 February 1842. But a few days later he took to his bed for two weeks, complaining to Grzymala, 'My mouth and tonsils are aching so much.' After this, he did not perform again in public for six years.

At times, it seems as if he used his music to defy his situation, for nothing could be more brilliantly heroic than his A♭ major Polonaise, Opus 53, while the Fourth Ballade and Fourth Scherzo (his last in both genres) have a mysterious beauty and gaiety which were new in his music. All these date from 1842. Still to come were the great Sonata in B minor (1844), with its songfully elegiac slow movement and passionate finale, and the wonderful but poignant Polonaise-Fantaisie that he began in the autumn of 1845 but did not complete until the following summer – 'I don't know what to call it', he said. Also from 1846 are the sumptuous Barcarolle and his Cello Sonata in G minor written for his cellist friend Auguste Franchomme.

Of course, artists and Parisian society being what they were, some things changed. George Sand and Marie d'Agoult fell out, and although Liszt tried to ensure that this did not affect his friendship with Chopin, that did happen to some extent. In the meantime the relationship between Chopin and George fluctuated. She fussed over him in a way that he sometimes needed and sometimes resisted, writing to Grzymala in 1843 of her 'poor child ... I know he suffers without me ... I need to care for him as much as he needs my care'. His pupil Zofia Rozengardt

The 'players' at Nohant, including Chopin, Liszt, Delacroix and the Sand family in a drawing by Maurice Sand (Lebrecht)

sometimes found him difficult, 'petulant as a spoiled child' and then suddenly all charm and gentleness, 'a weird incomprehensible man'. Wilhelm Lenz said he had to treat Chopin 'like a lady whom he wanted to please'.

On 12 May 1844, he heard that his father had died in Warsaw, and shut himself away, grieving, for some days. Later this year, his sister Louise and her husband, a law professor, visited him in Paris and then, in August, joined him and George in Nohant, where, to George's surprise, she found Louise very likeable. Back in Paris during that winter, he sometimes had to teach lying on his sofa, smelling salts in hand, and was often in pain, but frequently music restored him. Two new pupils now joined him who were to become friends: one was Princess Marcelina Czartoryska, then in her mid-twenties and a fine musician, and the other was the forty-year-old Scotswoman Jane Stirling.

George had long noted his unpredictable touchiness during his visits to Nohant and declared, 'I must not let him think he is the master here.' By 1845, she felt free to have other love affairs, and their relationship inevitably changed. Other factors also helped this to happen: Maurice, now twenty-two, thought himself the master of Nohant and resented Chopin's place there. Though nothing was said, Chopin noticed his attitude and in turn became closer to his sister Solange, now seventeen; she seems to have played up to him, possibly to spite her mother. Matters were not helped when George adopted her cousin's daughter Augustine Brault, who seemed to Solange to usurp her mother's affections. The atmosphere became tense, but George, absorbed in her writing, may not have been aware of it.

None of this helped Chopin's work. At Nohant in July 1845, he finished his Three Mazurkas, Opus 59, but then became bored and listless, telling his sister,

Poet and friend, Adam Mickiewicz (Lebrecht)

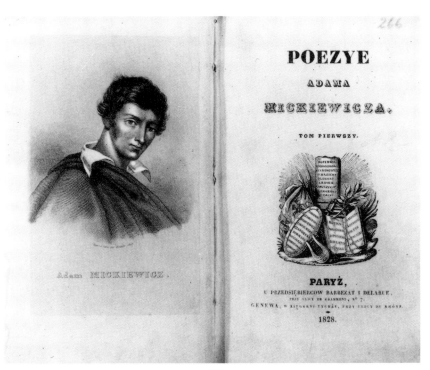

I'm not playing much, as my piano's gone out of tune, and I'm composing even less. I feel strange here this year ... I don't drink my morning chocolate, and I've moved my piano to a different place ... I'm not at all myself just now, only usually in some strange vacuum.

Yet in September, George wrote to him in Paris, 'Love me, my dearest angel, my dearest happiness, I love you.' He returned to Nohant for October and November, and George noticed that he was fairly well but 'worried, like all ill people, always burying himself in advance'. A bad sign was his increasing difficulty with composition, and he told his family, 'I can't write anything in winter.' Like his Polonaise-Fantaisie, his Cello Sonata and Barcarolle were started in this year but not completed until 1846.

During the winter, in Paris, he again had flu, but told his family, 'I've outlived so many younger and stronger people that I'm beginning to think myself immortal.' Friends called on him, including Liszt, Meyerbeer and his old Dresden acquaintance Auguste Klengel. He enjoyed evenings spent with Delacroix, Grzymala and the gifted young singer Pauline Viardot with her husband Louis. In April 1846, he stayed briefly with Franchomme's family near Tours, returning to Paris to give a musical evening at home for his friends, but at the end of May he was again in Nohant.

That June, George published her novel *Lucrezia Floriani*, telling of a famous actress living in her country home with the sickly, neurotic but exquisitely cultivated Prince Karol whom she nurses to health and with whom she falls in love;

A bust of the composer by George Sand's son-in-law, Clésinger (Lebrecht)

in the end, his difficult personality wears her out and she dies. At once people said that this was an obvious portrait of herself and Chopin, and undoubtedly it was, although she denied it. Delacroix was astonished when she read parts of the book aloud in Chopin's presence, and at his approving comments. The picture of Chopin as a succubus draining George's strength may be shocking, but it is fair to recall that this was how his friend Adam Mickiewicz saw this strange relationship. Others, of course, took the opposite view: for them, George Sand had to be the sinister force corrupting his genius.

In the same month of June, Maurice and Chopin quarrelled, and George took her son's side. Peace was restored, but the summer was uneasy and a heatwave took its toll on everyone's nerves. 'I do everything I can to work but it's no good,' Chopin told Franchomme in a letter; only the Three Mazurkas, Opus 63, date from this time. On 11 November, he returned to Paris.

Though he did not know it, this was the beginning of the end of his affair with George, which many had in any case expected after the appearance of *Lucrezia Floriani*: Liszt had written asking Marie d'Agoult, 'Is the break between Chopin and Madame Sand definite? And for what reasons?' In the meantime, Solange became engaged to a young man of good family and in February 1847 George arrived in Paris to arrange the wedding. But at this point, Solange fell in love with (and was seduced by) the much less suitable Auguste Clésinger, a sculptor, and they were married in May. In June a violent quarrel over money flared up at Nohant between the Clésingers and Maurice, during which Clésinger actually struck George. Expelled with her husband from the house, Solange wrote to Chopin begging the use of his carriage to return to Paris, and he agreed, at the same time telling George

The invitation to Chopin's last concert in Paris, 16 February 1848 (Lebrecht)

Soirée de Mr Chopin

dans l'un des Salons de Mrs Pleyel & Cie

20, Rue Rochechouart,

Le Mercredi 16 février 1848, a 8 heures ½

Rang   Prix 20 francs.   place réservée N.º 1

Pourtour.

that he had given his permission. Horrified that he should take the side of her daughter in this quarrel, George returned a furious letter; it has not survived, but Chopin showed it to Delacroix, who called it 'horrible. Cruel passions and long pent-up impatience erupt in it'.

After ten days, Chopin replied, suggesting that George's duty was still to support her daughter. But she was in no mood to accept a lecture and decided that Chopin's support of Solange betrayed a sexual attraction and thus also betrayed his benefactor, herself. She replied:

> *Very well, my friend, accept now the dictates of your heart and assume that it's the voice of conscience ... Look after her, then ... I've had enough of being a dupe and victim. I forgive you, and shall not utter a word of reproach ... Adieu, my friend ... I shall thank God for this strange ending to nine years of exclusive friendship. Let me hear sometimes how you are.*

Thus the pattern of his life changed again, and he spent the hot summer months of 1847 in Paris. It was a sad time, and even Grzymala, currently in financial difficulties, was small help. In November, he was shocked to hear of the death of Mendelssohn. But at the end of the year his friends persuaded him to give another concert; the Salle Pleyel's three hundred seats were advertised at twenty francs each, and the concert took place on 16 February 1848. He performed his Berceuse, Barcarolle and the 'Minute' Waltz (Opus 64 No.1), which was encored. He also joined Franchomme and the violinist Delphin Alard in a Mozart piano trio as well as performing the last three movements of his Cello Sonata. Why only three

Chopin by Delacroix; both were frequent visitors to Nohant (AKG)

movements? Perhaps he could not be sure of having the strength to play more; afterwards he nearly fainted in the artists' room. However, the concert was a triumph and the *Revue et Gazette Musicale* declared that only a Shakespeare could describe his playing, which was incomparable, while the Marquis de Custine wrote, 'You've gained both in suffering and in poetry ... preserve yourself for your friends' sake ... you are equal to your own genius, that says everything.'

Plans were already afoot for another concert on 10 March, but had to be abandoned when, on 22 February, Paris exploded in an uprising that dethroned Louis-Philippe; perhaps it was not surprising when a peasant's daily wage was a tenth of the price of a ticket for Chopin's concert. At any rate, it may have prompted him to accept an invitation to perform in Britain that came from his pupil Jane Stirling and her sister Mrs Catherine Erskine. On 20 April, he arrived in London, again at once noticing the local smog; rooms had been provided in Bentinck Street but he soon moved to Dover Street, near Piccadilly, where he had his Pleyel piano and two more that were loaned to him. He visited his friend the Count de Perthuis, then with the exiled French royal family at Kingston, and met a number of society and artistic people, including the novelist Charles Dickens and the historian Thomas Carlyle. Pauline Viardot was also there, and so were Sigismund Thalberg and the Swedish soprano Jenny Lind.

Chopin gave some lessons and played at a few private houses for a fee of twenty guineas, once at least before Queen Victoria, but turned down an invitation to play a concerto for the Philharmonic Society (he had not played with an orchestra for a long time, and probably thought that he no longer had the strength for it). Although he made money, living expenses consumed much of it, not least because he insisted on

*Chopin's pupil and hostess, Jane
Stirling (Lebrecht)*

A view of nineteenth-century London (AKG)

his high standard of living, with a valet, a rented carriage, and a daily visit from a hairdresser.

In July the London season ended, and he travelled north to Edinburgh, where he became the guest of Jane Stirling's elderly brother-in-law Lord Torphichen and again enjoyed every luxury, including the use of two fine pianos and the provision of the Paris papers. But he was unhappy and unwell, writing to Fontana, 'I can hardly breathe, and feel on the point of dying.' At the end of August he played at Crumpsall House, Manchester, before over a thousand people. As the Manchester *Guardian* observed, he appeared painfully frail but his performance belied his physical weakness. Returning to Scotland and further social activity, first with a resident Pole, Dr Adam Lyszczyński, and then with another Stirling relative, he soon became bored, telling Grzymala, 'I'm angry and miserable. People irritate me with their excessive care. I can neither rest nor work. I feel alone, alone, alone, although surrounded by people.' At Johnstone, a carriage accident, after its horses bolted, left him uninjured but shaken. He appreciated 'excellent pianos, beautiful pictures and choice libraries', but a further problem was Miss Stirling's increasingly pressing affection: we know from a letter to Grzymala (30 October) that he finally had to tell her that he could offer only friendship – 'I'm nearer the grave than to a bridal bed.'

The next day he set off for London, where he was examined by two leading doctors, one of whom (the Royal Physician, Sir James Clark) was an authority on tuberculosis who had treated the poet John Keats. They could only recommend an early return to Paris. Before he left London, he played on 16 November at a concert held in support of a Polish cause and partly organized by his old friend Princess Marcelina Czartoryska. But he longed to return, writing to Grzymala: 'One day

A daguerreotype of the composer taken in 1849, the year of his death (Lebrecht)

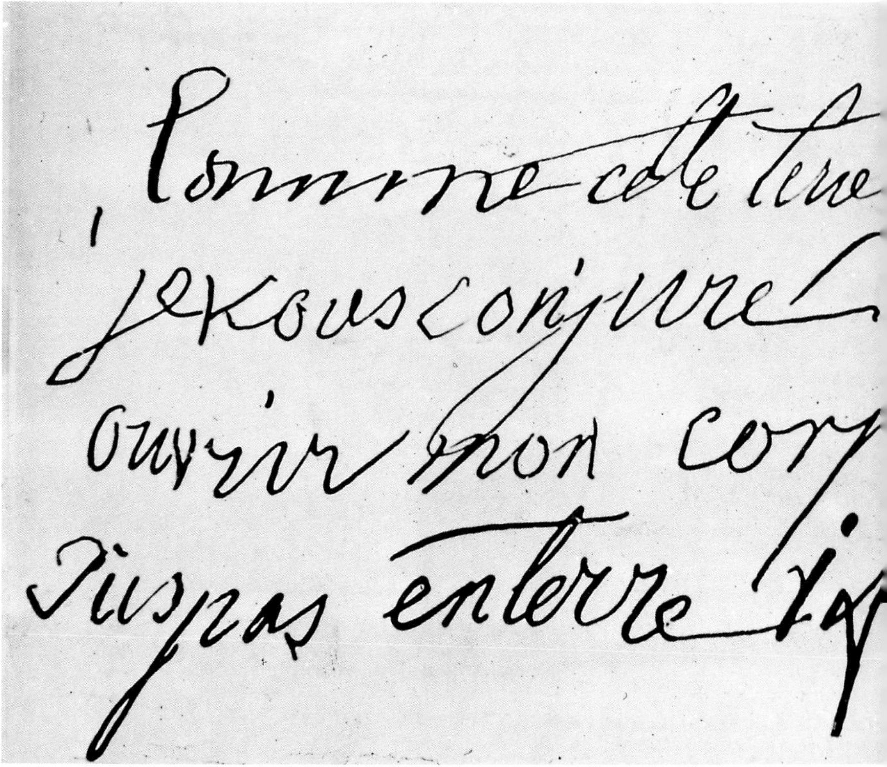

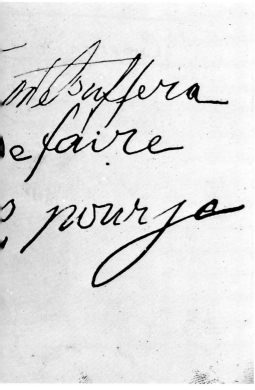

Chopin's last words, asking to make sure that he will not be buried alive (Mansell)

longer and I'll go mad.' On 23 November he left London with a travelling companion, Leonard Niedzwiedzski, crossed the Channel to Boulogne, where they spent the night, and arrived back in Paris the next day.

His principal doctor, the homeopath Dr Molin, had died earlier that year. He therefore called in others, but as he told Solange Clésinger in January 1849, 'they poke about but bring me small relief'. Invariably they prescribed rest, but he commented bitterly, 'I'll soon have rest without their help.' The spring sunshine made him feel better, but from now on he knew that he was going downhill. However, he still managed to teach a little, and his friends ensured that he was never lonely; Delacroix, in particular, went out of his way to bring company to the friend whom he called 'my poor great dying man', although sometimes he would find Chopin hardly able to breathe. He had fits of coughing and would spit out blood.

Though George was now out of his life, she could not remain indifferent to his fate and welcomed news of him, and Pauline Viardot wrote to tell her, 'He no longer goes out in the evenings, but still manages to give some lessons, and on his better days can be quite cheerful.' However, on 16 April he made an evening visit to the Opéra to see Viardot as Bertha at the première of Meyerbeer's *Le prophète*. In the following month, to avoid Paris's summer heat, his friends moved him to a cool and more spacious suburban apartment at 74 Rue de Chaillot; he wondered that the rent was so low, not knowing that half of it was paid by one of them. There he enjoyed a good view of Paris, but he was less happy when Jane Stirling and her sister installed themselves nearby and began wearying him with well-meant visits; Delacroix would have been better company, but he had left Paris and was wondering if they would meet again. However, he was grateful for a gift of money from Jane, who left a

Chopin on his deathbed, drawn by Kwiatkowski (Lebrecht)

packet of 25,000 francs in banknotes anonymously that nearly failed to reach him; when it did, he accepted 15,000 'as a loan'.

He was perhaps already trying to put his affairs in order, writing to Louise in Poland begging her to come, and adding, 'I'm ill and no doctor can help as much as you can.' Later he wrote to his old friend Tytus Woyciechowski, whom he had not seen for many years but who was passing through Belgium; Tytus could not visit Paris because the frontier was closed to 'Russian subjects', and Chopin told him, 'I wanted to set off for Valenciennes, at the frontier, to meet and embrace you, but I simply could not go.' In July, Delfina Potocka wrote from Aix-la-Chapelle, 'I cannot remain in the dark regarding your health ... God protect you, dear M. Chopin. I hope to see you at the beginning of October at the latest.' Someone else wrote to George, suggesting that she might visit him 'at this last stage of his long sufferings', but she replied that she felt unable to do so and had 'the conviction that he does not wish it'.

On 8 August, Louise and her husband reached Paris and hastened to his bedside. Now at last George decided to make an approach, writing to Louise asking for news, but she left the letter unanswered; it is not known if this was Chopin's wish. But other old memories were briefly renewed, for Delfina Potocka returned to Paris and Chopin invited her to visit and sing to him, which she did on 15 October.

In September Chopin had moved yet again, for his friends felt that he should be in a sunny apartment near the centre of Paris and easy to reach. But his condition had been deteriorating markedly for three months, and though they noted his tenacity and courage, it was clear that the end was approaching. A Polish friend who was a priest encouraged him to prepare for death by confessing and accepting

The model for Szymanowski's memorial to Chopin in Warsaw (Lebrecht)

extreme unction as a baptized Catholic, even though no longer a practising one, and after refusing several times he finally agreed and, afterwards, apparently said, 'Without you I'd have died like a pig!'

In his last days, there were always people at his bedside: they included his sister Louise, Solange Clésinger, Marcelina Czartoryska and his pupil Adolf Gutmann. On the evening of 16 October, they recited prayers to the sound of his laboured breathing, and the end came in the early hours of the following day.

Chopin's funeral took place on 30 October, at the Madeleine. The great church was packed with a congregation of three thousand, and Pauline Viardot and Louis Lablache were among the soloists in a performance of Mozart's Requiem, performed at the dying man's request. Chopin was buried in the cemetery of Père-Lachaise, with Prince Adam Czartoryski as the official chief mourner and Delacroix and Meyerbeer among the pall-bearers. Later, a casket of Polish earth was placed in the grave.

It has often been argued that Chopin's remains should be returned to Poland, but this has not yet been done, and on the whole it seems fitting that he should rest in his adopted country, France. In fact, he may be said to belong to the whole world. He was no hero, certainly, but great and heroic deeds are not only to be measured in obvious ways, and his work has proved more lasting and life-enhancing than the victories of an Alexander or a Napoleon. Schumann was right when he declared this extraordinary individual, who was also a creative genius, to be 'one of the proudest spirits of the age'. A century after his death, the pianist Arthur Rubinstein was to write, 'When I play Chopin, I know I speak directly to the hearts of people!'

The death mask of Chopin

chopin

the complete works

Most of Chopin's works are catalogued according to Opus (work) numbers and these are roughly based on the date of composition. The chronology of Chopin's works has been disputed but dates are given where known.

WORKS WITH OPUS NUMBERS

OPUS 1   Rondo, C minor (1825)

OPUS 2   Variations on 'Là ci darem la mano', B♭ major (1827)

OPUS 3   Introduction and Polonaise Brillante, C major (1929–30)

OPUS 4   Sonata, C minor (1827–8)

OPUS 5   Rondo à la mazur, F major (1826)

OPUS 6   Four Mazurkas, F# minor, C# minor, E major, E♭ major (1830–2)

OPUS 7   Five Mazurkas, B♭ major, A major, F major, A♭ major, C major (1st version of No. 4, 1825) (1830–2)

OPUS 8   Piano trio, G minor (1928–9)

OPUS 9   Three Nocturnes, B♭ minor, E♭ minor, B major (1830)

OPUS 10   Twelve Etudes (1830–2)

OPUS 11   Concerto No. 1, E minor (1830)

Opus 27	Two Nocturnes, C# minor, D♭ major (1835)
Opus 28	Twenty-four Preludes (1838–9)
Opus 29	Impromptu, A♭ major (c. 1837)
Opus 30	Four Mazurkas, C minor, B minor, D♭ major, C# minor (1837)
Opus 31	Scherzo, D♭ major (1837)
Opus 32	Two Nocturnes, B major, A♭ major (1837)
Opus 33	Four Mazurkas, G# minor, D major, C major, B major (1838)
Opus 34	Three waltzes:
	A♭ major (1835)
	A minor (c. 1834)
	F major (1838)
Opus 35	Sonata, B♭ minor (slow movement 1837) (1839)
Opus 36	Impromptu, F# major (1839)
Opus 37	Two Nocturnes, G minor, G major (1838–9)
Opus 38	Ballade, F major (1839)
Opus 39	Scherzo, C# minor (1839)
Opus 40	Two Polonaises, A major, C major (1838–9)

Four Mazurkas, E minor, B major, A♭ major, C# minor (1838–9)	Opus 41
Waltz, A♭ major (1840)	Opus 42
Tarantelle, A♭ major (1841)	Opus 43
Polonaise, F# major (1841)	Opus 44
Prelude, C# minor (1841)	Opus 45
Allegro de concert (c. 1834–41)	Opus 46
Ballade, A♭ major (1841)	Opus 47
Two Nocturnes, C minor, F# major (1841)	Opus 48
Fantaisie, F minor, A♭ major (1841)	Opus 49
Three Mazurkas, G major, A♭ major, C# minor (1842)	Opus 50
Impromptu, G♭ major (1842)	Opus 51
Ballade, F minor (1842–3)	Opus 52
Polonaise, A♭ major (1842–3)	Opus 53
Scherzo, E major (1842–3)	Opus 54
Two Nocturnes, F minor, E♭ major (1842–4)	Opus 55
Three Mazurkas, B major, C major, C minor (1843–4)	Opus 56

OPUS 57	Berceuse, D♭ major (1844)
OPUS 58	Sonata, B minor (1844)
OPUS 59	Three Mazurkas, A minor, A♭ major, F# minor (1845)
OPUS 60	Barcarolle, F# major (1845–6)
OPUS 61	Polonaise-fantaisie, A♭ major (1846)
OPUS 62	Two Nocturnes, B major, E major (1846)
OPUS 63	Three Mazurkas, B major, F minor, C# minor (1846)
OPUS 64	Three Waltzes, D♭ major, C# minor, Ab major (1847)
OPUS 65	Sonata, G minor (1845–6)
OPUS 66	Fantaisie-impromptu, C# minor (c. 1834)
OPUS 67	Four Mazurkas: G major (c. 1835) G minor (1848–9) C major (1835) A minor (1846)

Four Mazurkas:	OPUS 68
C major (c. 1830)	
A minor (c. 1827)	
F major (c. 1830)	
F minor (c. 1846)	
Two Waltzes:	OPUS 69
A♭ major (1835)	
B minor (1829)	
Three Waltzes:	OPUS 70
G♭ major (1832)	
F minor (1842)	
D♭ major (1829)	
Three Polonaises:	OPUS 71
D minor (1827–8)	
B♭ major (1828)	
F minor (1828)	
Three Ecossaises, D major, G minor, D♭ major (1828)	OPUS 72
Rondo, C major (1828)	OPUS 73

OPUS 74   17 Songs

1. 'Zyczenie' (Witwicki) (c. 1829)
2. 'Wiosna' (Witwicki) (1838)
3. 'Smutna rzeka' (Witwicki) (1831)
4. 'Hulanka' (Witwicki) (1830)
5. 'Gdzie lubi' (Witwicki) (c. 1829)
6. 'Precz z moich oczu' (Mickiewicz) (1827)
7. 'Posel' (Witwicki) (1831)
8. 'Sliczny chlopiec' (Zaleski) (1841)
9. 'Melodia' (Krasinski) (1847)
10. 'Wojak' (Witwicki) (c. 1831)
11. 'Dwojaki koniec' (Zaleski) (1845)
12. 'Moja pieszczotka' (Mickiewicz) (1837)
13. 'Nie ma czego trzeba' (Zaleski) (1845)
14. 'Pierscien' (Witwicki) (1836)
15. 'Narzeczony' (Witwicki) (1831)
16. 'Piosnka litewska' (Witwicki) (1831)
17. 'Spiew grobowy' (Pol) (1836)

WORKS WITHOUT OPUS NUMBERS

Polonaise, B major, K. 1182–3 (1817)

Polonaise, G minor, K. 889 (1817)

Polonaise, A♭ major, K. 1184 (1821)

Introduction and variations on a German air ('Der Schweizerbub'),
E major, K. 925–7 (1824)

Polonaise, G# minor, K. 1185–7 (1824)

Mazurka, B♭ major, K. 891–5 (1825–6)

Mazurka, G major, K. 896–900 (1825–6)

Variations, D major, K. 1190–2 (1826)

Funeral March, C minor, K. 1059–68 (c. 1826)

Polonaise, B♭ minor, K. 1188–9 (1826)

Nocturne, E minor, K. 1055–8 (1827)

Souvenir de Paganini, A major, K. 1203 (1829)

Mazurka, G major, K. 1201–2 (1829)

Waltz, E major, K. 1207–8 (c. 1829)

Waltz, E♭ major, K. 1212 (1830)

Mazurka, G major, K. 1201–2 (1829)

Waltz, A♭ major, K. 1209–11 (1830)

Waltz, E minor, K. 1213–4 (1830)

K. 1204–6 (1830)

Polonaise, G♭ major, K. 1197–1200 (1829)

Lento con gran expressione, C# minor, K. 1215–22 (1830)

Grand Duo concertant on themes from Meyerbeer's 'Robert le Diable', E minor, K. 901–2 (1831)

Mazurka, B♭ major, K. 1223 (1832)

Mazurka, D major, K. 1224, 1st version K. 1193–6 (1832)

Mazurka, C major, K. 1225–6 (1833)

Cantabile, B♭ major, K. 1230 (1834)

Mazurka, A♭ major, K. 1227–8 (1834)

Prelude, A♭ major, K. 1231–2 (1834)

Variation No. 6 in Hexameron, E major, K. 903–4 (1837)

Trois Nouvelles Etudes, K. 905–17 (1839–40)

Canon, F minor, K. 1241 (c. 1839)

Mazurka 'Notre Temps', A minor, K. 919–24 (c. 1839)

Sostenuto (Waltz), E♭ major, K. 1237 (1840)

Dumka, K. 1236 (1840)

Fugue, A minor, K. 1242 (c. 1841)

Moderato, E major, K. 1240 (1843)

Two Bourrées, G minor, A major, K. 1403–4 (1846)

Largo, E♭ major, K. 1229 (1847)

Nocturne, C minor, K. 1233–5 (1847)

Waltz, A minor, K. 1238–9 (1847)

chopin

recommended recordings

The following list of recordings is included as a guide to some of the interpretations of Chopin's work available at the time of writing and is by no means intended as an exhaustive catalogue. The works are listed first, followed by details of the recording: the artists, record company and disc number. All numbers given are those that apply to the compact disc format, but many recordings can also be bought on conventional tape cassette.

Solo Piano Music

Albumblatt in E major

Allegro de concert

Opus 46   Barcarolle

Opus 60   Berceuse

Opus 57   Boléro

2 BOURRÉES	OPUS 19
CANTABILE IN B♭ MAJOR	
CONTREDANSE IN G♭ MAJOR	
3 ÉCOSSAISES	OPUS 72/3
FUGUE IN A MINOR	
GALOP MARQUIS	
LARGO IN E♭ MAJOR	
MARCHE FUNEBRE	OPUS 72/2 3
TROIS NOUVELLES ÉTUDES	
RONDOS	OPUS 1, 5, 16, 73
SONATA NO. 1 IN C MINOR	OPUS 4
TARANTELLE	OPUS 43

OPUS 12	VARIATIONS BRILLANTES
	VARIATION NO. 6 FROM HEXAMERON
	VARIATIONS ON A GERMAN NATIONAL AIR
	VARIATIONS (SOUVENIR DE PAGANINI)
	[1]VARIATIONS FOR PIANO DUET
OPUS 74/2	[1]WIOSNA FROM
	Vladimir Ashkenazy; [1]with Vovka Ashkenazy. Decca 421 035-2(2).
OPUS 45	ALLEGRO DE CONCERT
	BALLADES NOS. 1–4

INTRODUCTION & VARIATIONS ON JE VENDS DES SCAPULAIRES   OPUS 12
Hamish Milne.
CRD CRD 3360.

BALLADES NO. 1–4

SCHERZI NOS. 1–4
Artur Rubinstein.
BMG/RCA RD 89651 [RTCD1 7156].

Vladimir Ashkenazy.
Decca 417 474-2.

ÉTUDES   OPUS 10/1–12

ÉTUDES   OPUS 25/1–12

Trois Nouvelles Études
Louis Lortie.
Chan. Dig. CHAN 8482.

Opus 10/1–12	Études
Opus 25/1–12	Études
	Polonaises 1–7
Opus 28	24 Preludes
	Maurizio Pollini.
	DG 431 221-2 (3).
Opus 60	Barcarolle
Opus 57	Berceuse
Opus 49	Fantaise in F minor
Opus 29	Impromptu No. 1 in A♭ major
Opus 36	Impromptu No. 2 in F# major

Impromptu No. 3 in G♭ major   Opus 51
Murray Perahia.
Sony Dig. MK 39708.

Mazurkas Nos. 1–51
Vladimir Ashkenazy.
Decca 417 584–2 (2).

Nocturnes Nos. 1–21
Vladimir Ashkenazy.
Decca 414 564-2 (2).

Claudio Arrau.
Ph. 416 440-2 (2).

Polonaises Nos. 1–7
Artur Rubinstein.
BMG/RCA RD 89814 [RCA 5615-2].

Shura Cherkassy.
DG 429 516-2; 429 516-4.

Opus 28   24 Preludes

              Preludes Nos. 25-26

              Impromptus Nos. 1-4

Opus 66   Fantaisie-impromptu
              Claudio Arrau.
              Ph. 426 634-2; 426 634-4.

Opus 28   24 Preludes
              Maurizio Pollini.
              DG 413 796-2.

Opus 28   24 Preludes

Opus 59   Preludes Nos. 25-26

Opus 39   Scherzo No. 3 in C# minor
              Martha Argerich.
              DG 431 584-2; 431 584-4.

Sonata No. 2 in B♭ minor (Funeral march)	Opus 35
Andante spianato et Grande Polonaise brillante	Opus 58
Études	Opus 10/3–4
Nocturne No. 8 in D♭ major	Opus 27/2

John Bingham.
Mer. ECD 84070; KE 77070.

Piano sonatas No. 2 in B♭ minor	Opus 35
Piano sonata No. 3 in B minor	Opus 58

Mitsuko Uchida.
Ph. Dig. 420 949-2; 420 949-4.

Piano sonata No. 2 in B♭ minor	Opus 35
Barcarolle in F# major	Opus 60
Polonaise No. 6 in A♭ major (Heroic)	Opus 53

OPUS 61   POLONAISE-FANTAISIE IN A♭ MAJOR
Martha Argerich.
DG 431 582-2; 431 582-4.

OPUS 35   PIANO SONATA NO. 2 (FUNERAL MARCH)

OPUS 58   PIANO SONATA NO. 3 IN B MINOR

OPUS 49   FANTAISIE IN F MINOR
Artur Rubinstein.
BMG/RCA RD 89812 [RCA 5616-2-RC].

OPUS 35   PIANO SONATA NO. 2 IN B♭ MINOR (FUNERAL MARCH)

OPUS 58   PIANO SONATA NO. 3 IN B MINOR
Murray Perahia.
Sony CD 76242 [MK 37280].

OPUS 59   PIANO SONATA NO. 3 IN B MINOR

Ballade No. 4 in F minor	Opus 52
Barcarolle	Opus 60
Mazurkas	Opus 59/1-3
Polonaise-Fantaisie	Opus 61

Peter Katin.
Olympia OCD 186.

Waltzes Nos. 1–14
Artur Rubinstein.
BMG/RCA RD 89564 [RCD1-5492].

Waltzes Nos. 1–16.
Peter Katin.
Decca 417 045-2; 417 045-4.

Waltzes Nos. 1-14	Opus 60

Opus 50/3	Barcarolle
Opus 27/2	Mazurka in C# minor
	Nocturne in D# major
	Dinu Lipatti.
	EMI CDH 7 69802-2.
Opus 23	Ballade No. 1 in G minor
Opus 60	Barcarolle
Opus 66	Fantaisie-Impromptu
Opus 7/1	Mazurka in B♭ major
Opus 33/2	Mazurka in D major
Opus 9/2	Nocturne in E♭ major
Opus 15/2	Nocturne in F# major

NOCTURNE IN D♭ MAJOR	OPUS 27/2
NOCTURNE IN G MINOR	OPUS 37/1
POLONAISE IN A MAJOR (MILITARY)	OPUS 40/1
POLONAISE IN A♭ MAJOR	OPUS 53
WALTZ IN A♭ MAJOR	OPUS 34/1
WALTZ IN D♭ MAJOR (MINUTE)	OPUS 64/1
WALTZ IN C# MINOR	OPUS 64/2

Artur Rubinstein.
BMG/RCA GD 87725 [7725-2-RG]

BALLADE NO. 1 IN G MINOR	OPUS 23
FANTAISIE-IMPROMPTU	OPUS 66
MAZURKA IN B♭ MAJOR	OPUS 7/1

Opus 33/2	Mazurka in D major
Opus 9/2	Nocturne in E♭ major
Opus 15/2	Nocturne in F♯ major
Opus 32/1	Nocturne in B major
Opus 53	Polonaise in A♭ major
Opus 31	Scherzo in B♭ minor
Opus 18	Waltz in E♭ major (Grand valse brillante)
Opus 34/2	Waltz in A minor
Opus 69/1	Waltz in A major
Opus 69/2	Waltz in B minor
Opus 70/1	Waltz in G♭ major
	Vladimir Ashkenazy.
	Decca Dig. 417 798-2; 417 798-4.

BALLADE NO. 3 IN A♭ MAJOR	OPUS 47
BARCAROLLE IN F# MAJOR	OPUS 60
FANTAISIE IN F MINOR	OPUS 49
FANTAISIE-IMPROMPTU	OPUS 66
NOCTURNE NO. 2 IN E♭ MAJOR	OPUS 9/2
NOCTURNE NO. 5 IN F# MAJOR	OPUS 15/2
PRELUDE IN D♭ MAJOR	OPUS 28/15
WALTZ NO. 7 IN C# MINOR	OPUS 64/2
WALTZ NO. 9 IN A♭ MAJOR Claudio Arrau. Ph. 420 655-2; 420 655-4.	OPUS 69/1
ÉTUDES NO. 3 IN E MAJOR, NO. 5 IN G♭ MAJOR, NO. 12 IN C MINOR (REVOLUTIONARY)	[1]OPUS 10

[2]Opus 25   No. 9 in G♭ major

[3]Opus 66   Fantaisie-impromptu

[3]Opus 9/2   Nocturne No. 2 in E♭ major

[2]Opus 32/2   No. 10 in A♭ major

[4]Opus 40/1   Polonaise No. 3 in A major

[5]Opus 53   Polonaise No. 6 in A♭ major (Heroic)

[6]Opus 28   Prélude No. 7 in A major, No. 20 in C minor

[7]Opus 18   Waltz No. 1 in E♭ major (Grande valse brillante)

[7]Opus 64/1-2   No. 6 in D♭ major (Minute); No. 7 in C# minor
[1]Anievas; [2]Adni; [3]Ogdon; [4]Ohlsson; [5]Pollini; [6]Orozco; [7]Malcuzynski.
CfP CD-CFP 4501; TC-CFP 4501.

CHAMBER MUSIC

PIANO TRIO IN G MINOR   OPUS 8
Trio Fontenay.
Teldec/Warner Dig. 2292 43715-2.

CELLO SONATA IN G MINOR   OPUS 65
Du Pré, Barenboim.
EMI CM57 63184-2.
Miklós Perényi, Tibor Wehner.
Hung. White Label HRC 171.

Concertante and Orchestral Music

[1] Opus 1   Piano concerto No. 1.

Opus 22   Andante spianato et Grande polonaise brillante

Opus 18   Waltz No. 1 in E♭ major (Grande valse brillante)
Krystian Zimerman, [1]with Royal Concertgebouw Orch. of Amsterdam,
Kondrashin.
DG 419 054-2; 419 054-4.

[1] Opus 1   Piano concerto No. 1

Opus 38   Ballade No. 2 in F major

Opus 54   Scherzo No. 4 in E major
Krystian Zimerman, [1] with Royal Concertgebouw Orch. of Amsterdam,
Kondrashin.
DC Analogue/Dig. 431 580-2; 431 580-4.

Opus 1   Piano concerto No.1 in E minor

PIANO CONCERTO NO. 2 IN F MINOR   OPUS 21
István Székely, Budapest Symphony Orch, Gyula Németh.
Naxos Dig. 8.550123.

Zimmerman, Los Angeles PO, Giulini.
DG415 970-2.
Rubinstein, London New Symphony Orch, Skrowaczewski.
BMG/RCA RD 85612.

PIANO CONCERTO NO. 2 IN F MINOR   OPUS 21
Ashkenazy, LSO, Zinman.
Decca 417 750-2.

LES SYLPHIDES (ballet; orch. Douglas).
Philadelphia Orch, Ormandy.
Sony SBK 46550

National PO, Bonynge.
Decca Dig. 430 723-2; 430 723-4.

AAM *Academy of Ancient Music*
arr. *arranged/arrangement*
ASMF *Academy of St. Martin–in–the–Fields*
attrib. *attributed*
bar. *baritone*
bc. *basso continuo*
bn. *bassoon*
c. *circa*
ch. *chorus/choir/chorale*
Chan. *Chandos*
cl. *clarinet*
CO *Chamber Orchestra*
COE *Chamber Orchestra of Europe*
comp. *composed/composition*
contr. *contralto*
db. *double bass*
DG *Deutsche Grammophon*
Dig. *digital recording*
dir. *director*
ECO *English Chamber Orchestra*
ed. *editor/edited*
edn. *edition*
ens. *ensemble*
fl. *flute*
HM *Harmonia Mundi France*
hn. *horn*
hp. *harp*
hpd *harpsichord*
Hung. *Hungaroton*

instr. *instrument/instrumental*
kbd. *keyboard*
LSO *London Symphony Orchestra*
Mer. *Meridian*
mez. *mezzo-soprano*
ob. *oboe*
OCO *Orpheus Chamber Orchestra*
orch. *orchestra/orchestral/orchestrated*
org. *organ/organist*
O-L *Oiseau-Lyre*
perc. *percussion*
pf. *pianoforte*
picc. *piccolo*
PO *Philharmonic Orchestra*
qnt. *quintet*
qt. *quartet*
sop. *soprano*
str. *string(s)*
tb. *trombone*
ten. *tenor*
tpt. *trumpet*
trans. *translated/translation*
transcr. *transcribed/transcription*
unacc. *unaccompanied*
va. *viola*
var. *various/variation*
vc. cello
vn. violin

- SELECTED FURTHER READING -

G Abraham, *Chopin's Musical Style* (London, 1939)

A Boucourechliev, *Chopin: A Picorial Biography* (London, 1963)

C Bourniquel, *Chopin* (London, 1960)

M Brown, Chopin: *An Index of His Works* (London, 1960)

A Heldey, *Chopin* (London, 1964)

A Heldey, *Selected Correspondence of F Chopin* (London, 1962)

G Marek & Gordon Smith, *Chopin* (New York, 1978)

F Niecks, *F Chopin as Man and Musician* (London, 1888)

A Walker, *Frédéric Chopin: Profiles of the Man and Musician* (London, 1966)

A Zamoyski, *Chopin* (London, 1979)

- ACKNOWLEDGEMENTS -

The publishers wish to thank the following copyright holders for
their permission to reproduce illustrations supplied:

Archiv Für Kunst und Geschichte, London
Lebrecht Collection
Private Collection, Lebrecht Collection
The Mansell Collection Ltd

1. **WALTZ NO. 1 IN E♭ MAJOR, OP. 18 5'17"**
Nikita Magaloff
This vigorous yet lilting waltz became one of the most famous numbers in the ballet Les Sylphides, *based on Chopin's music and first given in St Petersburg.*

2. **MINUTE WALTZ 1'42"**
Nikita Magaloff
Brief though this is, its popular name is misleading, for it cannot be squeezed into sixty seconds without sounding rushed. It has also been called the 'Little Dog' Waltz, because its whirling figures suggest a puppy chasing its tail.

3. **PIANO CONCERTO NO. 1, ADAGIO 11'18"**
Claudio Arrau, London Philharmonic Orchestra/Eliahu Inbal
The rich lyricism of this youthful work shows Chopin's astonishing melodic gift as well as his total understanding of the piano.

4. **BALLADE NO. 1 IN G MINOR, OP. 23 9'28"**
Nikita Magaloff
One of the most dramatic of Chopin's works, alternating 'storm and stress' with eloquent melody.

5. **ÉTUDE NO. 1 IN C MAJOR, OP. 10 2'07"**
Nikita Magaloff
Brilliant right-hand arpeggios here rise and fall above a striding, heroic bass line. So difficult is this piece that pianists say they need 'danger money' to play it in public.

6. ÉTUDE NO. 3 IN E MAJOR, OP. 10   4'24"
   Nikita Magaloff
   A study in melody playing with one of the composer's loveliest tunes, once made into a song called 'So Deep is the Night'. The middle section, however, is surprisingly forceful.

7. NOCTURNE NO. 8 IN D♭ MAJOR, OP. 27/2   5'57"
   Nikita Magaloff
   The dreamy evening atmosphere here is typical of Chopin's nocturnes, as is the way the music rises to a climax before the peaceful close.

8. PRÉLUDE NO. 17 IN A♭ MAJOR, OP. 28   3'56"
   Nikita Magaloff
   This somewhat Italianate piece makes full use of the sustaining pedal to create sumptuous sonorities.

9. IMPROMPTU NO. 4 IN C# MINOR, OP. 66   5'29"
   Nikita Magaloff
   Chopin wrote this in 1835 but, for some reason, never published it. Today it is one of his most popular pieces. The melodious middle section is based on the same rising figure as we hear in the agitated opening.

10. POLONAISE NO. 6 IN A♭ MAJOR, OP. 53   6'29"

Nikita Magaloff

Heroic nationalism is the keynote of this great polonaise with its galloping middle section.

11. MAZURKA NO. 1 IN G MINOR, OP. 24   2'37"

Nikita Magaloff

Though a dance, this mazurka is quiet and pensive, featuring the rhythmic flexibility called rubato.

12. MAZURKA NO. 4 IN B♭ MINOR OP. 24   4'03"

Nikita Magaloff

Another beautiful, passionate but somewhat enigmatic piece, whose rocking opening figure sounds curiously modern in harmony.

13. PIANO SONATA NO. 2, MARCHE FUNÈBRE   7'17"

Nikita Magaloff

Written two years before the other movements of the Second Sonata, this celebrated funeral march begins and ends in the deepest gloom although the gentle middle section is consoling.

"The ideal way to discover more about favourite composers"

Woman and Home

**This revolutionary package of book and compact disc, produced in association with Philips Classics and Classic FM, is the ultimate prelude to the lives and works of the most popular composers of classical music.
Each volume is priced at £9.99 (inc. VAT).**

These books may be ordered by post direct from the publisher.
Please contact the Marketing Department.
But try your bookshop first.